BEAUTIFUL DAY
FORTY YEARS OF IRISH ROCK

BEAUTIFUL DAY
FORTY YEARS OF IRISH ROCK

SEAN CAMPBELL AND GERRY SMYTH

ATRIUM

For our families

First published in 2005 by
Atrium
Youngline Industrial Estate
Pouladuff Road,
Togher
Cork, Ireland

Atrium is an imprint of Cork University Press

British Library Cataloguing in Publication Data
A CIP catalogue record for this book is available from the British Library.

ISBN 0-953535-355

Typeset and designed at bitedesign.com

Printed by Butler & Tanner Ltd, Somerset

Contents

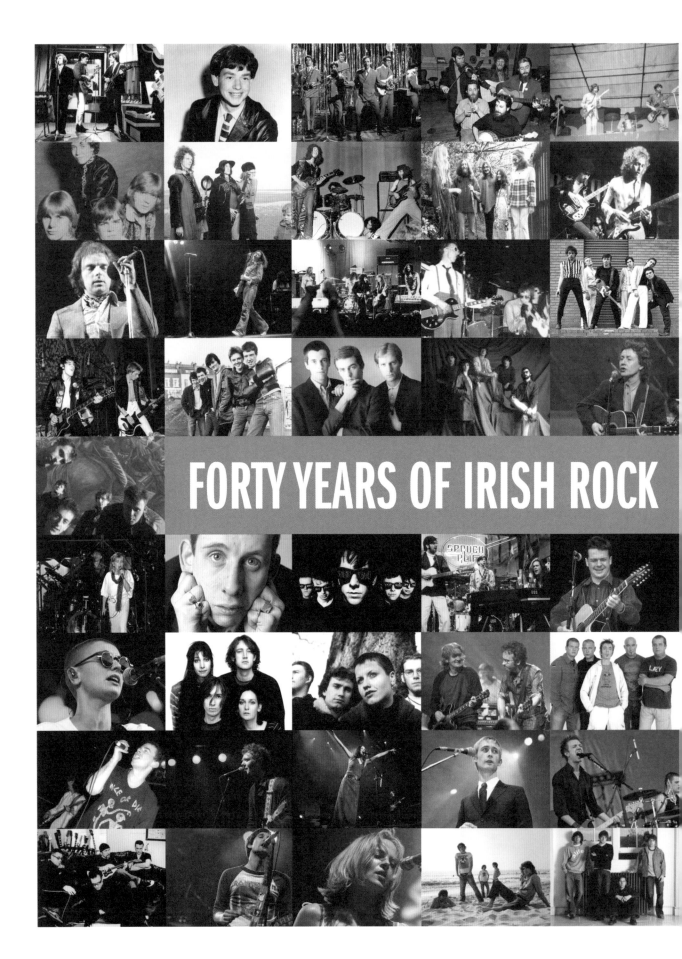

FORTY YEARS OF IRISH ROCK

Acknowledgements

Our thanks go to all the friends who have in one way or another contributed to the writing of this book: Steve Averill, Neil Badcock, Samantha Ball, Stuart Borthwick, Candida Bottaci, John Braine, Paul Burton and Emma-Jane Rosenberg, Cambridge University Library, Fergus Campbell, Margaret Campbell, the Campbells of Thurles and Naas, Lucy Collins, Mike Collins, Anton Corbijn, Cork Campus Radio, Cathal Coughlan, Colin Coulter, Ross Dawson, Alan Downey, Anne and Steve Fisher and family, John Fisher, Simon Fletcher and Carine Augoyard-Fletcher, Ian Gallagher, Andy Gee, David and Fiona James, the Jordans of Co. Galway, Francis Kennedy, Leah Loughnane, the Loughnanes of Chicago and Indiana, Davy Lutton, Colm McAuliffe, Martin McLoone, Jonathan Moore, Stephen Moulton, Ron Moy, Regine Moylett, Killian Murphy, Tony Murray, Mick O'Keefe, Damian O'Neill, Ivan Pawle, Ondrej Pilny, François Pittion, Steve Pyke, Graham Runacus, (Faculty of Arts at APU, Cambridge), Jon Savage, George Smyth, Kevin Smyth, Bill Sweeney, Billy Webster, Paul Webster, Roger Woolman and Stephen Wright. We would especially like to thank Sara Wilbourne former Publisher of Cork University Press.

Introduction

THE BACKGROUND

They say the Irish are a musical race, and they've been saying it for years. In his first-hand account of the conquest of the island during the late twelfth century, religious type and imperial apologist Giraldus Cambrensis – who had practically nothing good at all to say about Ireland or the Irish – reluctantly acknowledged the musical prowess of the natives, writing: 'It is only in the case of musical instruments that I find any commendable diligence in the people. They seem to me to be incomparably more skilled in these than any other people that I have seen.'

This essentially British notion of some kind of 'natural' link between Irish identity and music continued to develop after this time. It played an especially important role in the complex colonial relations of the eighteenth and nineteenth centuries. At certain times and in certain contexts it suited all sides in the colonial nexus – Gaelic Ireland, Anglo-Ireland, and imperial Britain – to push this line, and to inflect it in particular political directions.

For the British, the Irish penchant for music was typical of the Celt's propensity for cultural pursuits; the concomitant of this, of course, was the Celt's unsuitability for material concerns. This amounted to saying: 'You get on with the poetry – we'll come and listen when we can – but in the meantime we've got this business to run.' For the Anglo-Irish, music was a supposedly 'neutral' cultural arena wherein they could indulge their 'Celtic' tendencies without endangering the attitudes or practices which underscored their political domination. For the Irish, meanwhile, music became a form of compensation for material dispossession, a simultaneous remembering and forgetting, a rare transport of delight in what was for the vast majority of them a more or less uniformly dismal world.

A useful definition of ideology is that it seeks to convert culture into nature, to make us accept the invented as the real. In this sense it's clear that the notion of the Irish as a musical race was (and remains) an ideological proposition, invented and developed over time to expedite a specific political dispensation. Now, it is the case that over an extended period of history music did become a significant aspect of island culture for a variety of identifiable social and political reasons; but this is not the same thing as saying – or believing – that the Irish simply *are* a musical race.

Nevertheless, this idea continued to impact upon Irish cultural practices in the years leading up to the revolution of the early twentieth century, and in the decades which followed. Forty years after the revolution, however, it would be tested by the advent of a new set of practices based, on the one hand, on certain trends within twentieth-century American (and especially African-American) popular music and, on the other, on an aesthetic principle that ran somewhat at odds with Irish music's heavy reliance on the notion of tradition: the principle of creative self-expression. The Irish were still officially a 'musical' race in the early 1960s, but not every kind of music was amenable to the national character. So, a new question needed to be asked: Was Ireland ready to *rock?*

Well, it all depends on what you mean by 'Ireland' and what you mean by 'rock'. Thinking about the subject of 'Irish rock' is always going to be difficult because both elements of the formulation have been undergoing constant change ever since it was first broached as an artistic and cultural possibility. The island of Ireland has been the site of a great number of overlapping tendencies – social, cultural, economic, political – in the forty years between 1964 and 2004. You could explain the changes that have occurred in any number of ways; as useful as any description, however, is the claim that both parts of the island have gone from being aspirationally modern to enthusiastically postmodern within a single generation. That's quick by anyone's standards, and it has created a situation in which it's very difficult to know which 'Ireland' is actually being invoked at any given time or in any given context. The difficulty is compounded when you realize that during the exact same period rock music has been evolving exponentially.

We don't want to labour the point here. As a working premise, however, it doesn't seem to be claiming too much to say that there exists a crucial relationship between a society's popular music and its wider social, cultural and political make-up. This book is in part an attempt to tell the stories of the changes that have overtaken both 'Ireland' and 'rock music' since the early 1960s and, more precisely, to consider the mutual impact of each of these stories upon the other. That examination, moreover, takes place within the context of the 'special' relationship between Irishness and musicality described above – in other words, when we engage with Irish rock music we should expect it to be inflected, at the levels of both production and consumption, by an older discourse which claims that Irishness and music are essentially, although mysteriously, linked.

THE MUSIC

Rock 'n' roll music first began to impact upon Ireland in the late 1950s and early 1960s. Once there, it met and cross-bred with a number of other practices to produce the strange Frankenstein creature that history remembers as the showband. Originally, showbands were groups of musicians who toured the island (and later abroad) playing a range of popular musical and dance styles. These musicians did not compose their own music; their appeal lay, rather, in their evocation of the twin values of *accuracy* and *entertainment* – which is to say, they attempted to reproduce the music they played (including quite centrally the popular rock 'n' roll hits of the day) as accurately as possible, while the prevailing ethos of their performances was one based upon entertainment. Especially influential in rural areas, the showbands became enormously popular, often playing to relatively huge audiences in different parts of the country several times a week. An entire industry – encompassing venue construction, magazine and record production, management and technical infrastructure, as well as a huge pool of musicians – very quickly grew to support them. The heyday of the showbands may have been the 1960s, but it's fair to say that they introduced a set of values which continues to impact upon Irish popular musical practices down to the present day.

Another key genre that emerged in Ireland during the 1960s was traditional music. Although this kind of music had been 'popular' with many people at home and abroad throughout the twentieth century, during this particular decade two specific influences – one technological, the other cultural – combined to bring it to the forefront of the Irish cultural imagination. The first encompassed the manufacture and dissemination of cheap playback media (including radio and television), which had the effect of greatly increasing the potential audience for performances of traditional music, and the electrification of acoustic instruments. The second was the advent of folk music as an international cult, and its association (however opportunistic and/or tendentious) with a number of high-profile figures, of whom the most influential was Bob Dylan. The purists might argue (and did, ad nauseam) over the precise nature of the relationship between 'folk' and 'traditional' music. Whatever the truth, one of the effects of the folk boom was to convert Irish traditional music over a period of time from a primarily *past*-oriented practice – in which the reiteration of the tradition was the key impulse – to a set of increasingly *present*- and *future*-oriented practices associated with discourses of authenticity and technical expertise which have proved attractive to successive generations of young Irish people.

Alongside the showband and trad movements, Ireland began to develop an alternative scene based in the first instance on the success of the 'Merseybeat' sound and played by what were referred to at the time as 'beat groups'. Although there was much overlap – in terms of personnel, instrumentation and sometimes sound – between 'beat', 'show' and folk/trad music, these groups were different in a number of important respects: they did play a lot of covers, but generally of material that they regarded to be more progressive, 'cooler' than that played by the showbands; they began to write their own songs; there tended to be fewer band members; their sound was dominated by guitars and keyboards, and the use of brass instruments was a rarity; they helped develop an alternative gig circuit; they were less successful in financial terms; they were, at least nominally, more interested in the music than the business; dancing was a side rather than a central issue during performance; they were future- rather than past-oriented; they were internationalist.

In fact, what the music of groups such as The Greenbeats, The Strangers, The Chosen Few and The Chessmen represented was the first expression in Ireland of the rock ideal that was to feature so strongly in all subsequent thinking about popular music. As a second guiding principle we want to suggest that a defining characteristic of this rock ideal was that it offered young people important experiences – namely, self-realization through creative endeavour – by and large unavailable elsewhere in society. What we mean by this is that if showband music was animated in the main by discourses of *accuracy* and *entertainment,* and if traditional music was animated in the main by discourses of *authenticity* and *technique,* then beat music was animated in the main by a discourse of *creative self-expression* – that is, by the possibility of saying something original about the world as you apprehend it. This is not to deny that accuracy, entertainment, authenticity and technique have all played significant, frequently crucial, roles in the emergence of Irish rock music during the past four decades. But what rock brought to the mix, as it were, was the chance to speak *your* truth in your own voice, however amateurish, raw or far removed from society's prevailing narratives. And in societies such as the Republic and Northern Ireland in the early 1960s, where both the ability to speak and 'the truth' had been so effectively marshalled by the respective states and state religions for so long, this was an extremely attractive prospect.

Perhaps the major thing that rock music offered young Irish people in the early to mid-1960s, however, was the prospect of a connection with a group defined for the first time in terms of age rather than religion, race, class or gender – an international population of adolescents and young adults who, on the invitation of their post-war, market-oriented parents, had come to a sense of themselves as a unique social and cultural category. Encouraged to focus for so long on narrowly domestic issues, or disbarred entirely on account of their age, young Irish people grabbed the opportunity to register identification with an international youth culture and its defining noise: rock music.

We have neither the time nor the desire to risk a judgement regarding the precise ways in which changes in Irish leisure and lifestyle patterns – for example, greater travel opportunities, changes in education, the impact of television, and the general cultural glasnost pursued by leaders such as Lemass and Lynch in the south, and O'Neill in the north – engaged with the birth and subsequent growth of Irish rock music. Neither do we want to comment as to the socio-political provenance and/or the eventual fate of the Anglo-American baby-boomer generation with which Irish youth made sincere, if tactical, alliance. What may be claimed with reasonable confidence is that at some point during the 1960s rock music became an important aspect of the cultural imagination of young Irish people, and that it offered a range of experiences and affiliations which impacted significantly upon their processes of identity formation.

This, then, was the context within which an Irish rock tradition emerged and developed. Historically, there was the old story of 'the musical Irish', a story with which each new generation had to contend, regardless of genre, style or tradition. Culturally, there was the context of political and social change which made the time ripe for the emergence of a popular musical discourse organized around the principle of creative self-expression. Musically, there were other established practices – the showbands and traditional music – attempting to catch the ear of the Irish people. Once rock became an element within the island's musical imagination – once a part of the island's noise – there was no going back. There would be some unique developments, a few blind alleys and a number of blazing trails – but no going back. Rock was here to stay.

THE BOOK

On one level, this book is clearly another of those 'list' things with which every rock fan will be familiar. Making lists is something that rock writers and fans seem to be particularly fond of. Even a cursory survey of the field reveals that there's been a proliferation in recent years of publications which utilize the format of niche-market lists – in this case, books directed at special sections of the enormous popular-music market. A classic example is Ian MacDonald's *Revolution in the Head: The Beatles Songs and the Sixties* (1994), in which each song in The Beatles catalogue is discussed in turn. Or think about the tendency of rock publications such as *Q* and *Mojo* (not to mention television stations like VH1) to produce seemingly endless variations on the 'Top Ten', 'Top Fifty' and 'Top One Hundred.'

In fact, the list seems to have been one of the fundamental features of rock writing since the practice began back in the 1960s. This derives in part from the tendency amongst rock writers at all levels – from the most ambitious summarizer to the most humble reviewer – to compare different aspects of the rock tradition. Albums, songs, vocals, sounds, whatever, are described much of the time not in terms of *what they are*, but in terms of *what they are like*. While this reveals the writer's knowledge of the tradition on the one hand, on the other it contributes towards a general 'listing' mentality in which particular songs and sounds are clustered together in a variety of official and semi-official discourses. With reference to Irish rock music, for example, the trend is observable in the 'best of' or 'greatest' compilations that continue to appear from time to time. By the nature of the genre, such compilations invariably prove controversial, but this is seen as a bonus by those who produce them, as questions of what's included and omitted provide opportunities for interested parties from all aspects of popular music discourse (fans, musicians, commentators) to exercise their knowledge, taste and judgement, and thus to confirm their involvement.

But why do these lists appear, and why are we so interested in them? Our suspicion is that the practice is founded on a general tendency amongst rock fans (and perhaps amongst humans generally) to organize the material world into convenient mind-sized chunks which perform a number of important functions.

Firstly, they operate as a sort of shorthand for an entire outlook, enabling the fan to affiliate with the kinds of values that are associated with the items included in the list. Citing Van Morrison as one of your top-ten recording artists says something about the kind of person you are, as would the citation of The Nolans. The philosopher Martin Heidegger once said that we don't speak language, language speaks us. This is also the case with rock music. We don't choose it, it chooses us; we become the kind of listener, indeed, the kind of person who listens to a Van record or a Nolans record – *and all that that entails*. Measuring the distance between 'Madame George' and 'I'm in the Mood for Dancing' is one highly salient means by which large numbers of people in the modern world come to a sense of who they want and don't want to be.

Secondly, lists enable like-minded people to identify each other, and to cluster together in face-saving groups which avoid conflict while simultaneously confirming the validity of individual group members. As the great French music-theorist Jacques Attali writes: 'One consumes in order to resemble and no longer . . . to distinguish oneself.' Ever notice how metal fans, or punks or jazz heads tend to hang out together? Ever notice how they tend to look the same and speak the same, in some instances to *smell* the same? You don't *have* to have greasy hair and BO to like Motorhead, but it'll probably save a lot of hassle if you do. The tension and humour which can occur when music fans of different affiliations are obliged to associate may be observed in novels such as Roddy Doyle's *The Commitments* and Nick Hornby's *High Fidelity*.

Thirdly, it's just something to do, isn't it – a hobby into which you can pour some (and for some rock widows, far too much) of your disposable income and which occasionally gets you out in the evening. It may be a peculiarly male thing, and it may have something to do with certain changes in the meaning and role of masculinity in the late twentieth century, changes that more or less coincided with the success of rock as a popular musical form. This in turn may account for the overwhelming preponderance of men within rock music at every level – performance, industry, audience. Be that as it may, the original point remains: we all need stuff to do and to enjoy as a reward for the hard work we have to put into survival and to forget (at least temporarily) the downward physical and mental trajectory upon which we're all inevitably launched. We hope you knew this already.

The fact is that lists help us to survive in the modern world, and rock music offers us an accessible, complex and vast archive of materials from which to compile those lists. In identifying with various strands within this archive we also choose the values and meanings which are conventionally attached to them. So when the individual rock fan affiliates with a particular style or nominates a preference they not only adopt an identity, they also become part of a huge international community wherein such values and meanings are debated and decided.

Beautiful Day is a 'list' book that intervenes in the ongoing story of Irish rock music, considering some of the issues that attend it, and interrogating some of the assumptions that have emerged in relation to it. Besides this introduction, it's composed of forty-one entries, each of which is about 1,200 words in length and focuses on a particular song from each of the years between 1964 and 2004. The first date is the one at which something resembling a rock aesthetic began to make itself felt in Irish popular music-making practices. The over-riding principle throughout was to discuss one song a year which reflects upon or engages with wider socio-cultural trends and developments in late-twentieth- and early-twenty-first-century Irish society. Individual entries combine musicological, historical and cultural analyses in no particular ratio; some are more contextualized than others, some have more about the actual songs, some pick up on particular features or genres or trends, and so on.

This book should function as an introduction to the history of Irish popular music for those with little or no knowledge of the subject. At the same time, we wish to challenge the assumptions of those who are more familiar with the field. From the outset, a guiding criterion for inclusion of individual entries was *interest* rather than profile, popularity or success. Thus, the better-known names (Thin Lizzy, Van Morrison, U2 and so on) are all represented, but not necessarily by their most well-known or 'successful' recordings. In some instances, the best-known recording of lesser-known artists is included. All performers, no matter how successful, are allowed only one entry. Another guiding factor was our wish to provide a broad geographical representation of Irish popular music, rather than a narrowly Dublin-centred (or at least conurbation-centred) view. Likewise, we wished to confirm and recover, so far as possible, a strand of women's involvement in Irish rock. In all instances, however, we've been limited to some extent by the availability of material and by what must be acknowledged as the truth of the tradition: there's not much point in trying to recover the great Tralee rock scene if it in fact never existed; by the same token, there's little profit in looking for female performers in the first beat groups of the 1960s, because they're simply not there.

We anticipate a certain degree of crossover with some of those compilation and 'best of' texts alluded to above. However, whereas these are compiled in the main in terms of commercial and critical success, we're in pursuit of both a deeper and a wider analysis of Irish popular-music-making practices over the past forty years. There are a number of artists included here whose 'rock' credentials are more than a little suspect, but that's the point. What do *you* think rock music is, reader? Do *you* feel threatened or offended by the inclusion of certain artists or songs here, and if so, why? How far does this list confirm or challenge the story that *you* know, and to what extent are *you* yourself confirmed or challenged as a result?

In concluding, we acknowledge that we are as subject as any of the readers of this book to the processes described above. Trying to decide what to include and exclude was not an easy process. For good or bad, the decisions have left us publicly exposed in terms of our tastes, prejudices, critical assumptions and undoubted oversights. Another time, another place and another set of writers, and any of the following brilliant acts – more or less arbitrarily selected from the past forty years – could have replaced any of the ones included in *Beautiful Day.* So, thanks (and sorry) to: The Atrix, Auto Da Fe, Azure Days, Bell XI, Blue In Heaven, Cactus World News, The Capitol Showband, Chant Chant Chant, Mary Coughlan, Damien Dempsey, The Devlins, An Emotional Fish, Engine Alley, Fatima Mansions, Five Go Down To The Sea?, The Fountainhead, The 4 Of Us, The Frank And Walters, The Freshmen, Gavin Friday, Future Kings Of Spain, The Golden Horde, Granny's Intentions, The Greenbeats, A House, The Jimmy Cake, The Johnstons, Katmandu, Brian Kennedy, David Kitt, Jack L, Les Enfants, Light A Big Fire, Sinead Lohan, Melaton, Christy Moore, Moving Hearts, Samantha Mumba, Mundy, The Outcasts, The Pale, Picturehouse, The Prayer Boat, Protex, Damien Rice, Rubyhorse, Rudi, Ruefrex, Scullion, Some Kind of Wonderful, Something Happens, The Stars of Heaven, The Stunning, The Subterraneans, The Sultans of Ping, Sweeney's Men, Therapy?, Those Nervous Animals, Tír Na nÓg, Pierce Turner, The Virgin Prunes, and Andy White.

Gerry Smyth
Sean Campbell

1964

Gloria

THEM [DECCA]

No one will ever be able to determine the precise number and range of factors that came together in Ireland in the early 1960s to enable the emergence of what history remembers as 'beat' music. Some people maintain that the genre appeared as a result of lazy showbands paying smaller (in terms of size and reputation) groups a few pounds out of their own considerable earnings to play until the ballrooms filled up after pub-closing time. Others claim that radio (the BBC, Radio Luxembourg and American Forces Network) fed a desire – instigated during the Second World War, and especially prevalent to the east and north of the island – for American blues-based popular music. To these must be added stints abroad by disaffected showband members such as George Ivan Morrison and Liam Rory Gallagher, and the cultural horizons broadened thereby. In any event, by the summer of 1964, the rumblings of an alternative music-making practice were beginning to be heard all around the country, but nowhere more so than on the nascent Belfast club scene.

The complex genealogy of Them has been well documented – one critic has reckoned that they had at least nine different line-ups between 1964 and 1966. Even more than their American contemporaries The Byrds, Them were not so much a 'group' in the Beatles tradition – a tight, organic unit composed of a relatively small number of friends – as a space through which a pool of performers constantly moved in the service of a musical ideal represented by the band name. In many ways, the constantly changing personnel that characterized Them's career is indicative of their basis in a rhythm 'n' blues (and also, by association, jazz) aesthetic as opposed to that of the pop 'group'. Throughout the band's long and decreasingly successful life, it was always *supposed* to be the music – hard-nosed, beat-driven, electric rhythm 'n' blues, with the occasional foray into folkish territories – rather than the personalities that mattered. In retrospect, we can see that despite his own convictions regarding the integrity of the music and his suspicion of the personality cults so assiduously promoted by the modern popular music industry, Van Morrison was always the key to the band's sound and success. Given the tension between *his* talent and the musical ideal to which the band ostensibly subscribed, it was perhaps inevitable that a personality as large as his would need to find a discrete platform sooner rather than later.

But this is to get beyond ourselves. We know that Morrison, having packed it in with The Monarchs, formed Them with guitarist Billy Harrison in the winter of 1963, and the best sources reckon that by the time of their residency in Belfast's Maritime Hotel and their first London recording session in the summer of 1964, the line-up was completed by Eric Wrixon on organ, Ronnie Millings on drums and Alan Henderson on bass. If the musical complement was reminiscent of The Animals (whose 'House of the Rising Sun' was topping the charts on both sides of the Atlantic as the men from Northern Ireland were in the recording studio), Them were probably closer in image and ethos to their Decca label-mates The Rolling Stones, who scored a big summer hit with 'It's All Over Now', and who (along with The Beatles, The Animals and The Yardbirds) were in the vanguard of the so-called 'British Invasion' of North America. That Them are routinely name-checked in this narrative is not inappropriate (their influence over a generation of American garage rockers is in fact well documented) – and not only because they were indeed technically 'British'; in musical terms, and certainly in terms of the band's self-identity, they really did belong with those outfits rather than with the ones churning it out in the ballrooms of romance. Even the band's confrontationally blue-collar name was an indication of how far they had travelled in their collective imagination from the Royals, Capitols and Monarchs of this world.

Controversy still surrounds the issue of who actually played the signature guitar riff on the A-side of Them's breakthrough single, 'Baby, Please Don't Go' (1964). Apparently, top session man and future rock god Jimmy Page was never far away during the band's London sessions; and although they played electrifying live sets, there were serious questions as to Them's studio technique. Except for the most retentive of completists, the point must remain moot. In any event, riveting though that track is, it has been eclipsed in rock history by the record's B-side. 'Gloria' is 2 minutes and 36 seconds of primal garage rock that – more than transformations on the economic, political or religious fronts – announced the arrival of a new stage in modern Irish history, and stands as an entirely suitable point of departure for a book about the history of Irish rock music.

In 1964 the island north and south was in the process of emerging from its long dark night, but many shadows still lay across the land – shadows of a politics which insisted that geography was destiny, of a religious system conceived in the name of love but practised in hatred, of a suspicious economic management class and of a culturally conservative populace. It would be fair to say that this era got the popular music it deserved in the showbands, which, for all their undoubted fun and excitement, were officially 'onside' in terms of image, outlook and general attitude towards the societies in which they flourished. It may be difficult to appreciate forty years down the road, but 'Gloria' represented a profound threat to the ruling castes of those societies and their self-aggrandizing monopoly on prevailing moral standards. And as so often, the threat, when it came, was cast in terms of the most fundamental and most heavily policed aspect of human experience: sex.

As with the blues material upon which they are based, many of the Van-penned Them songs are about the alienation and heartache that accompany loss of love. Odd, then, that his first great songwriting achievement should be one in which the guy gets

Best Bit: The build up of tension as the eponymous heroine makes her way via street, house, door, towards 'my' bedroom – what will she do to make me feel 'alright'?

the girl in such brazenly sexual terms. The sneering, triumphant vocal combines with a stomping uptempo rhythm (in which every beat is accented equally) to create the sense of a powerful, energetic masculinity. 'Gloria' is the reverse side of 'Baby, Please Don't Go' in more ways than one; just as the latter laments the spatial removal of the love object (to New Orleans) so 'Gloria' tracks the girl's advance towards the boy's room in scintillatingly provocative detail. This coming together in spatial terms serves as a metonym for the 'coming together' of sexual congress, an act which is itself suggested in the musical build-up beginning at 1.25, followed by the climactic surge as the chorus returns.

In medieval music, the key of E major signified heaven; this E-based rhythm 'n' blues belter, introducing one of the classic chord sequences in modern popular music, encapsulates the heaven of teenage sex, in which pleasure (so we've been told) lies as much in the anticipation as in the achievement.

You Turn Me On

BLUESVILLE [CAPITOL]

In 1965, the showbands were at the peak of their popularity, with groups such as The Capitol, The Dixies, The Drifters and of course the über-successful Royal Showband continuing the music- (and money-)making ways which had served them so well for so comparatively long. Although the showbands were not solely a rural phenomenon, it's fair to say that their bread and butter was the extensive ballroom circuit outside Dublin and the other main conurbations. In the cities, meanwhile, things had been tending in a significantly different direction. Fed by two overlapping trends in contemporary British popular music – the rhythm 'n' blues movement on the one hand, and the explosion of 'beat' music on the other – a genuine alternative music scene had begun to emerge. The different spatial locale of this scene was a reflection of its spiritual and imaginative distance from the ballroom circuit and the kind of music that thrived there.

But in what specific ways did the showbands differ from emerging beat groups such as The Greenbeats, The Chosen Few, The Chessmen and (the focus here) Bluesville? Numerous empirical factors can be (and have been) cited: the urban/rural biases already mentioned; the relative size of the typical outfits; the dress codes and instrumentation of each; the emphasis on 'show' in the one as opposed to that on expression in the other; the maintenance of an 'orchestral' aesthetic amongst the showbands as opposed to the emphasis on a basic bass- and kit-driven beat music; and so on. Rather than functioning as one or other *cause* of the split, however, these factors should be seen as representative *symptoms* of a fundamental change that was overtaking Irish-popular music-making practices at this time. This change, in turn, was itself part of a wider social revolution, a revolution which, determined by worldwide political and economic trends, had been making itself felt in Irish life since the turn of the decade.

By 1965, a properly planned economic recovery was well in hand. Of greater symbolic importance, perhaps, was the Republic's entry that year into a Free Trade Agreement with the United Kingdom, and the exchange of official visits between Seán Lemass and Terence O'Neill, respective leaders of the southern and northern states. These developments signalled that at least some people in Ireland were willing to step out from the shadow of the past and accept the reality of life in the late twentieth century. If that reality in the main consisted of changes in media consumption, the 'logic' of European economic integration, and a Cold War politics inspired by the competing ideologies of the US and the USSR, it also connoted a revolution in leisure and lifestyle trends. And it's here (believe it or not) that we find the basis of the split between the showbands and the beat groups.

Around about 1955, American rock 'n' roll (drawing on trends and tendencies deep within American cultural history) introduced the notion of an authentic, youth-oriented music that was in its essential form divorced from the concerns and interests of older generations. This basic idea evolved in some interesting ways in the following years, for example, the penchant amongst so many white middle-class English boys for the various blues-based musics produced during the twentieth century by a wide variety of African-American performers. These boys were interested in 'keeping it real' an entire generation before hip hop's vainglorious battle cry was heard. In the meantime, when this rock 'n' roll ethos began to make itself felt in Ireland, its adherents found in the showbands a handy example of all they considered to be inauthentic and 'unreal'. It was the difference (so they believed) between music as a business and music as its own reward, a difference which could be quantified in some of the ways cited above but which ultimately came down to intangibles such as taste, aura and atmosphere. Like most revolutions, subsequent events have proved the division to be misconceived. In Ireland in 1965, however, the battle line was clear, and which side you found yourself on said as much as anything else could about who and what you were.

It may seem a long way from the Bay of Pigs to Bluesville, but it's interesting to think that they might be locked into the same historical matrix. The latter was made up of Trinity College mates Ian Whitcomb, Barry Richardson and Peter Adler (yes, *that*

. . . .

Best Bit: Whitcomb's chicken impression during the chorus: 'And when, when you do ... ahuh, huh, huh, huh, huh, huh, there's my song!'

. . . .

Adler), plus local boys Deke O'Brien, Mick Molloy and Ian McGarry. In various guises and combinations, most of these names would continue to play a part on the Dublin beat scene for many years to come. The exception would be the expatriate Whitcomb, one of those aforementioned English boys for whom music simply *was* America. Under his charismatic leadership, Bluesville had been playing the burgeoning Dublin beat scene since 1963 when, thanks to a summer trip to Seattle, the band scored a remarkable US Top Ten hit in June 1965 with an original song entitled 'You Turn Me On' (aka 'You Really Turn Me On').

No less than any other band in the days before *Pet Sounds* (1966) and *Sgt. Pepper* (1967), Bluesville were caught in a dilemma when it came to recording. In 1965, no rationale existed for any kind of rock 'n' roll-derived product other than the 7-inch, sub-3-minute vinyl recording (or, in the case of the long-player, a collection of such recordings). Bluesville were thus committed to the aesthetics of the *song* rather than the *record* – which is to say, once in the studio, the band attempted to *reproduce* their live sound rather than *produce* a piece of independent art fashioned in response to the available studio technology. However, the technology at the Eamonn Andrews Studios in Henry Street, Dublin, where 'You Turn Me On' was recorded, was pretty basic even for 1965. As a result, Bluesville were not able to reproduce on vinyl the energy and commitment for which their live performances were famous. They were compelled, in other words, to record a song as an extension of their stage identity, but when it came to it, they couldn't really do that song justice.

The wonder is that, like so many of their peers working in similar circumstances, Bluesville managed to produce such a classic 1960s pop song. 'You Turn Me On' is a jaunty work-out in F, enlivened by some tight piano playing and nifty syncopation in the latter part of the track. What really makes it stand out, however, is Whitcomb's 'novelty' vocal – a stuttering falsetto which, as much as any specific musical affiliation (the band were considered part of 'the British Invasion'), probably accounted for its success in the US. Besides its basic blues-derived rock 'n' roll structure, Bluesville's many and varied influences can also be discerned on the track. Whitcomb was an enthusiastic student of popular-music history (something borne out by his subsequent career as music historian and presenter of legendary BBC rock show *The Old Grey Whistle Test*), and alongside the classic Jerry Lee Lewis riff which drives the song, he has cited American performers Jimmy Yancey and Champion Jack Dupree as inspirations for the band's sound.

We could speculate further regarding the song's structure and sound, the influence and role of Bluesville on the Irish beat scene, and the nature of the relationship between beat music and the showbands. The point is this, however: 'You Turn Me On' stands as evidence of a new phase in Irish popular-music-making, symbolizing the winds of change that by 1965 were already beginning to blow away fifty years of cultural cobwebs. The religious and civic leaders who complained about this new variation of 'the devil's music' had every right to be worried.

1966

Come Back to Stay

DICKIE ROCK [PYE]

Rock by name ... eh, something else by nature. Actually, this is an economical selection in as much as it provides us with an example of two popular-musical practices which ran parallel to the modern Irish rock tradition, and which continue to exercise an influence down to the present: the showbands and the Eurovision Song Contest.

We've already remarked the preponderance of the showbands during the 1960s. One such group was The Miami, who first emerged around 1963 and were (in various line-ups) at the forefront of the scene for the next dozen years. Their lead singer was a rake (the allusion is to size rather than promiscuity) from Cabra in north Dublin with the serendipitous surname of 'Rock'. Never as exciting as Brendan Bowyer (of The Royal), nor as dynamic as Joe Dolan (of The Drifters), nor anywhere near as handsome as Butch Moore (of The Capitol), Dickie nevertheless had the right stuff to amount to a star in his own country. In fact, Rock represented the Irish showband ethos in perhaps its purest form, for although he clearly wouldn't have turned down international success, he recognized from an early point that there was no harm in swimming in a small Irish pool as long as you were one of the biggest fish in it.

Dickie Rock has been one of the great survivors of Irish popular music, a successful showband performer, recording artist and cabaret entertainer in turn. Generations of knicker-flinging females can't be wrong; at the very least, nobody should dismiss the enduring appeal of an artist who has scored more Irish No. 1s than anybody else. He epitomized the attraction of the showbands – a lo-fi, non-threatening popular music, formally oriented towards the live performance of Anglo-American genres and thematically oriented towards working-class notions of fun and romance. When the plain people of Ireland wanted to step out in a modern style, Dickie was the man.

'Come Back to Stay' won the national song contest, held at the RTÉ studios on 22 January 1966. Dickie actually had three entries in the twelve-song competition, and beat the likes of Sonny Knowles and Butch Moore (who had represented Ireland on its Eurovision debut the previous year). The song came joint fourth in Luxembourg a few months later, and Dickie's celebratory return to Dublin Airport probably represented the peak of his forty-year career. (His triumph was unfortunately upstaged the following day when the IRA blew up Nelson's Pillar, a relic of British imperial rule in the centre of Dublin.) And as everyone knows, Eurovision's annual cheese-fest has continued to loom large in the Irish musical legend ever since, with seven wins and numerous high

placings making the country the most successful in the contest's history. Looking at the list of entries since 1965 – the Sean Dunphys and Red Hurleys and Linda Martins – you notice the prevalence of artists who in one way or another qualify as showband performers. The Eurovision and the showbands, in other words, appear to have been made for each other.

It may have all become a bit of an embarrassment, but it would be a mistake to underestimate the importance of the Eurovision Song Contest in modern Irish popular music history. When Ireland first opted to compete in 1965, it was one of a number of signals that the country was awakening from its long cultural hibernation; in particular, it was an acknowledgement of Ireland's dependence on the cultural and political future of Europe, and a small stepping stone to full membership of the Common Market. Dana's victory in 1970, and that of Johnny Logan ten years later, were especially significant events, signalling a measure of high-profile, popular success for which the national psyche was unprepared. It was only when the rest of the continent started to take the piss by electing three Irish champions running (1992–4) that people started to question seriously if Eurovision success was an accolade that anybody really wanted (or, as Fathers Ted and Dougal discovered, could afford).

In fact, the changing nature of Ireland's relationship with Eurovision, and particularly the high degree of showband participation, raises some key questions for modern Irish cultural history. Dickie's entry in 1966 roughly coincided with a hugely significant moment in the evolution of a 'serious' modern rock aesthetic. In terms of Irish popular music, the effect of this mutation was such that a clear divide emerged between the competitive ethos of the Eurovision – the idea that you could quantify your response to a piece of music, and that such a response would have material consequences – and the creative ethos of beat and rock bands, for whom love of the music was ostensibly the primary consideration. Of course, after Zappa, Bowie and (in an Irish context) U2's *Pop* (1997), we know this to be an artificial bourgeois divide based on the idea of a romantic artist spontaneously expressing deep emotions with which other less talented folk can somehow identify. (This is the cultural context in which Eurovision has gained such kitsch cred in recent years, especially amongst the continent's gay community.) Ireland's evolving relationship with the Eurovision is in fact a mirror of its evolving cultural consciousness, one in which showband values – once so central – increasingly came to be engaged only in satirical or nostalgic terms.

What of the song itself? 'Come Back to Stay' is a big ballad, a genre with which Rock has had much success over the years. The showband scene was large and diffuse enough to support a number of sub-traditions; although they might become identified with one particular song family or musical style, most artists maintained a repertoire of material from different popular genres, including rock 'n' roll, country and western, novelty pop, traditional Irish and romantic ballad. And although Dickie's name seemed to suggest that he might be located within the rock 'n' roll wing, he was best known in fact as a bit of a crooner. Throughout his career he always aspired more towards what he considered to be the 'professional' performance values of Frank, Deano and

Tony, as opposed to the (supposedly) rough 'n' ready rock 'n' roll values of Elvis, Buddy or Chuck.

Like many of its vintage, 'Come Back to Stay' doesn't go down too well these days. It is in fact a very poor man's 'Unchained Melody', a song which had been a big hit in 1965 for the Phil Spector-produced Righteous Brothers. Although Dickie couldn't hope to emulate Bobby Hatfield's spectacular vocals (he does in fact sustain a credible high E at the end of the song), and although the Irish recording industry was more than a few bricks short of Spector's famed 'wall of sound', there was some serious 'borrowing' going on, in terms of chord sequence, tempo, scoring and lyrics. Dickie's callow opening line – 'My love, I need your touch, I need your love so very much' – echoes the classic beginning of 'Unchained Melody': 'Oh my love, my darling, I hunger for your touch'. But it's just not the same. Dickie was thin in more ways than one; his material is a pale imitation of 'the real thing', while his delivery lacks the gravitas that only a long, deep tradition of popular entertainment can produce. Listening to the two tracks – ostensibly dealing with the same subject, and structured and delivered in a similar way – you begin to get some impression of the distance between these different musical realities: the gauche, self-deluding reality of the showbands, on the one hand, and the mature, technologically enhanced reality to which they aspired, on the other.

Best Bit: The end.

Seven Drunken Nights

THE DUBLINERS [MAJOR MINOR]

It's the Summer of Love and five hairy guys are singing about sex, infidelity and substance abuse on *Top of the Pops.* It's not The Rolling Stones or The Grateful Dead, however, but The Dubliners. And the fact that 'Seven Drunken Nights' was a song by an Irish folk group as opposed to an English or American rock band reveals a lot about prevailing cultural tendencies and political traditions in that revolutionary decade. Just as Dickie singing 'Come Back to Stay' stands in for an entirely different popular-musical tradition running parallel to (as well as overlapping at several key points with) modern Irish rock, so the inclusion here of what remains The Dubliners' most famous song acknowledges the ongoing impact that folk and traditional music have had on the emergence and development of Irish rock over the past four decades.

Irish traditional music played an important role in official state ideology after the revolutionary period at the outset of the twentieth century. This kind of music (itself diverse in form and dispersed in origin) was identified – along with various other things such as the Irish language, extensive literary and architectural remains, agricultural practices and GAA sports – as evidence of an ongoing, organic culture which had been interrupted by British colonialism but was now firmly back on line under a recovered Irish polity. Traditional music, in other words, provided the soundtrack for a bourgeois nationalist revolution, while also contributing significantly to the widespread notion of the Irish as an inherently musical race.

Around the beginning of the 1960s, however, traditional music began to interact with a related though distinct folk tradition that was making significant impact in the US and the UK. Besides its emphasis on the guitar ballad, the major influence that British and American folk music appears to have had was to dissipate the missionary aura that so often attended Irish traditional music. Suddenly it was cool to play ethnic, acoustic-based music, or at least music that leaned on that tradition. In Ireland, bands such as Sweeney's Men and The Johnstons began to challenge the institutional boundaries with which various state-sponsored ideologues had attempted to demarcate and police a set of supposedly discrete cultural practices. Such bands were, after all, made up of attractive young people whose lifestyle and appearance owed more to a contemporary international counter-culture than they did to the vision of Davis, Pearse or de Valéra. It's a reflection of the times, as well as a tribute to the fecundity of the tradition, that the boundaries so assiduously constructed by previous generations proved unequal to the task of containing the music.

All told, there's been a complex interplay between folk, traditional and rock music in Ireland since the 1960s, a relationship which has rendered bands like Planxty and Clannad, as well as individuals such as Christy Moore and Sharon Shannon, something of a music-store manager's nightmare. Even hardcore bona fide traditionalists such as The Chieftains have found it expedient to mix it up on a regular basis with artists from alternative traditions – Irish-derived and international, acoustic and electric. By the same token, rock musicians are not chary when it comes to recruiting traditionalist expertise in pursuit of certain effects associated with the music. Besides Horslips (who we will encounter in a later entry), Irish musical genre-bending finds perhaps its ultimate expression in Moving Hearts. Critically acclaimed though financially

· ·

Best Bit: The two 'missing' verses which creative listeners may (and frequently do) write for themselves.

· ·

unfeasible, this 'supergroup' was founded by Christy Moore in 1981 and featured at one time or another many well-known 'crossover' musicians (Donal Lunny, Davy Spillane and Declan Sinnott, amongst others). Moving Hearts played an eclectic mix of folk, rock, traditional and jazz. It's true that they were also widely regarded as a Republican group, thus seemingly underpinning the link between traditional music and conservative politics. In retrospect, however, it's clear that the band's particular brand of left-wing politics had more in common with the international *counter*-culture than with the hegemonic national culture, and that the interest of musicians such as Lunny and Moore was in the creative juxtaposition of different traditions rather than the fetishistic rehearsal of just one, supposedly discrete, national tradition.

The Dubliners were in at the ground floor of the folk boom in Ireland. 'The Ronnie Drew Folk Group', as they were first known, grew out of a regular session run in O'Donoghue's pub in Merrion Row on Dublin's south side in the early 1960s. The Dubliners had already recorded (for Transatlantic Records) and gone through a break-up and reformation by the time they came to record an album entitled *A Drop of the Hard*

Stuff for the Major Minor label early in 1967. The opening track on the album – also earmarked as the first single – was recorded 'live' in one studio take and featured Ronnie Drew singing in that 'coke-crushed-under-a-door' voice which, even more than Luke Kelly's powerhouse rasp, became the band's signature sound.

'Seven Drunken Nights' is based on an old Scottish ballad entitled 'Our Goodman', first noted by the collector David Herd in his two-volume *Scots Songs* (1776). It's also included in one of the most important pieces of folk research ever conducted, Francis James Child's *English and Scottish Popular Ballads* (1882–98), in which it features as entry number 274. Second only in popularity to 'Barbara Allen', over 400 versions of 'Child #274' have cropped up throughout the world – in English and other languages – pointing to the universality of its comic cuckold theme. More interestingly for our purposes, 'Our Goodman' is also suspected to be the only Child Ballad to have made its way into the blues tradition, with artists such as Blind Lemon Jefferson ('Cat Man Blues') and Sonny Boy Williamson ('Wake Up Baby') recording risqué versions in their own styles. When you remember the influence that artists such as these had on a whole generation of 1960s rockers, you start to get some idea of the way in which musical themes – both lyrical and sonic – persist over diverse times and places.

The Dubliners learned their version of the song in the early 1960s from Seosamh Ó hÉanaí (Joe Heaney). This revered *sean-nós* singer and storyteller from Galway had returned temporarily to folk-boom Ireland after many years in the UK, and associated with Drew and the rest of the band during their O'Donoghue's days. Ó hÉanaí may have heard an English-language version of the song during his time as a building labourer in Scotland in the 1940s, although a version of it had already made its way into the Irish ballad repertoire (itself heavily indebted to the English tradition) he learned during his Connemara youth. (The great American folklorist Alan Lomax recorded a version by Colm Keane in Galway in 1950.) In any event, The Dubliners released their version as a single on St Patrick's Day 1967, only to immediately fall foul of the state's antiquated censorship laws. Banned in Ireland (despite an appeal to Taoiseach Jack Lynch), the record was picked up by the pirate station Radio Caroline (founded by Irishman Ronan O'Rahilly), and saturation airplay led to a surprise hit in the UK charts shortly thereafter. The record sold proportionately well in Ireland, yet another clear signal to the keepers of the flame that the times they were indeed a'changin'.

In the final analysis, perhaps the chief values that traditional and folk music have lent to Irish rock over the years have been those of technique, tradition and attitude. Though somewhat deficient in respect of the first, and not a little opportunistic in terms of the second, The Dubliners always had ganseyloads of the third, and it's this as much as anything else that warrants their inclusion here.

Three Jolly Little Dwarfs

ORANGE MACHINE [DERAM]

If you weren't reading this book, and if you thought about it for a little while, you could probably make a pretty good guess as to the kind of music performed by a band called 'Orange Machine'. The clues are there in the colour reference and its ironic conjunction with something traditionally regarded as functional and banal. If you discovered that the band's heyday was the late 1960s your suspicions would be confirmed – Orange Machine were indeed what their name suggested them to be: a fully-fledged psychedelic rock band who during their short life displayed all the characteristics – musical and otherwise – of that much-loved and much-derided genre.

Of course, in Ireland the colour orange has special connotations, while 'orange machine' sounds like a phrase culled from a Gerry Adams' speech. Due to the high profile it adopted in relation to the Troubles, the Orange Order became one of the most recognizable forces in Ulster politics in the latter part of the twentieth century. In this context, it's interesting to note that the Orange political machine came into force in Northern Ireland in the same year (1968) in which 'Orange Machine' was leading the Irish response to the international phenomenon of psychedelia. In light of this, some questions perhaps worth asking are: were these two developments related, and if so, how?

In August 1966 a little-known band from Texas released an album entitled *The Psychedelic Sounds of the 13th Floor Elevators,* at which point the kind of music that left-field rock musicians had been making throughout that year finally had a name. Lysergic acid diethylamide, aka LSD or simply acid, had been welcomed in the US in the 1950s as a contribution to the relief of certain forms of mental illness. The word 'psychedelic' had been coined in 1957 to describe the sensations reported by the guinea pigs who had tried it. When acid was adopted by the American counter-culture as part of a general consciousness-raising programme, however, it quickly excited the fear and loathing of an increasingly defensive US establishment. The drug's take-off as the defining emblem

of the decade's counter-culture and its numerous fellow travellers (including rock musicians) may be dated more or less from the period of its ban by the US Federal Government in late 1965. Building slowly throughout 1966, the drug-inspired music finally came into its own in 1967, when it provided the soundtrack for the so-called Summer of Love.

Although a far from pure example of the genre, The Beatles' *Sgt. Pepper's Lonely Hearts Club Band* (1967) provided the spark that lit the fuse in the UK; thereafter, the genre developed apace, led by the band who were recording their debut album (*The Piper at the Gates of Dawn*) in another part of the Abbey Road studios at the same time as The Beatles were working on *Pepper*. British psychedelic music *à la* (The) Pink Floyd was on the whole more experimental and less politically oriented than its American counterpart. One thing they did share, however, was a love of colour – indeed, colour was perhaps the predominant characteristic of the psychedelic fashion that overtook popular culture on both sides of the Atlantic during 1967. The swirling tones and paisley patterns which featured in so much psychedelic art were an attempt to reproduce the experience of a good acid trip in which normal forms and definitions (allegedly) meld into each other. In this context, colour became (as it has done at various times throughout history) a radical counter-cultural response to non-representative authority, and an attempt to reclaim the magic of everyday life from the besuited 'man' and his monochrome vision of the world.

As had been happening since the 1950s, Ireland only discovered this new music some time after its advent elsewhere. Orange Machine emerged from an Irish beat scene which had thrown up local responses to most of the popular-musical fashions from the UK and the US, and which for its punters was located at some remove from both the showbands and the folk-trad boom. As a moniker, 'Orange Machine' referenced both psychedelia's penchant for bright colours and the influence of Soft Machine – in 1968 one of the British underground's vanguard bands. Their closest contemporary allies were the rather more successful and longer-lived Granny's Intentions, who also recorded for Deram (a subsidiary of major label Decca which specialized in more experimental music) and who, after scoring Irish hits with 'The Story of David' (1967) and 'Never an Everyday Thing' (1968), relocated to London. Both 'Three Jolly Little Dwarfs' and its B-side, 'Real Life Permanent Dream', were originally performed by another leading British psychedelic group, Tomorrow (the Irish band's second single, 'You Can All Join In', was also a cover of a Tomorrow song), whose enduring legacy was the psychedelic classic 'My White Bicycle' and who along with The Zombies figure as one of the best – and least-known – British bands of the period.

A bitter irony lies in the fact that just as Orange Machine were beginning to articulate an Irish response to psychedelic music, the 'revolution in the head' that it heralded was being brutally crushed. For if 1967 had given us the Summer of Love, 1968 was the Year of the Barricades, with student-led political disturbances throughout Europe and the US. Nineteen-sixty-eight was also the year in which a company of teenage US soldiers machine-gunned to death hundreds of people in the Vietnamese village of My Lai (March) and the year of Martin Luther King's assassination (April). Closer to home, it was also the year in which the Civil Rights movement in Northern Ireland was effectively hijacked by the sectarian discourses which have plagued the province ever since. You could say that at this time 'Orange Machine' – with all its playful, expansive, mind-freeing connotations – was displaced by an 'Orange machine' the task of which was to reproduce and disseminate its serious, foreclosed, suspicious view of the world.

'Three Jolly Little Dwarfs' was typical of the whimsical British response to psychedelia. Along with David Bowie's 'The Laughing Gnome' (April) and Pink Floyd's 'The Gnome' (August), it represents a sub-tradition of songs from 1967 about mythical small beings. Band members Ernie Durkan, Tommy Kinsella, Jimmy Greally and John Ryan produced a faithful version of Tomorrow's original, which had first appeared as a B-side to their failed 'Revolution' single. The original guitar line written by future Yes man Steve Howe remains just the acceptable side of twee, although the lyrics – concerning brightly dressed little guys prancing through meadows, sitting on toadstools and running away from giants – sound like a parody from an Austin Powers movie.

The song is tightly structured, however, and is certainly less fey than much of the material produced by contemporary Floyd. Modulating from the nursery-rhyme melody of the verse into more ambivalent territory in the bridge, the story told by 'Three Jolly Little Dwarfs' is the classic counter-cultural one concerning the destruction of idyllic innocence by a powerful, vindictive 'giant'. The 'very, very bright' sunshine of the day succumbs to the 'danger' lurking in the shadows of the night; the butterfly of joy is crushed upon the wheel of indiscriminate violence. All very hippy-dippy, of course. If the articulation was suspect, however, the instincts were sound, and in the case of Orange Machine's version, tragically prophetic.

Best Bit: As the 'giant appears' at 1.02 and 1.53, fuzzy lead guitar and vocals coalesce on an 'Indian' melody line that just screams 'I'm a psychedelic hippy, me'. Yeah, baby!!

Yes, I Need Someone

EIRE APPARENT [BUDDAH]

For many people, 1969 is the year in which an inescapable temporal logic began to take a specific spatial form on the island of Ireland, with the north representing 'the past' and the south 'the present'. The sectarian strife that had sparked into life in that part of the island over the previous years roared into full flame, taking almost everybody – including, perhaps, those most closely involved – by surprise. The province witnessed nothing less than a full-scale insurrection by the Nationalist minority, which in turn excited a military response from within the Loyalist community. That insurrection may have been pursued in the first instance in terms of a modernizing agenda which drew on the American Civil Rights movement and various other counter-cultural initiatives, but it was quickly overtaken by the resurgence of deeply atavistic values and perspectives, the consequences of which few could have imagined.

Down south, meanwhile, the widely touted civic and party-political revolution had, if not exactly withered on the bough, certainly failed to blossom to the satisfaction of many onlookers. A major strike by maintenance workers in the early part of the year, followed by the failure of the Labour Party's bid for a class-based politics and yet another Fianna Fáil election victory, paved the way for a period of doubt and misgiving which in turn would lead to recession and reaction. Few were in doubt that things had changed – if not utterly, then significantly – but to what end? Certainly, there was more money, more cars, more mod cons, more (and different) music – in short, more ... *stuff*. But what did all this stuff mean? What was it for? If the north was suffering from a surfeit of history, then the south appeared in danger of overdosing on a present which many felt amounted to little more than an unquestioning embrace of multinational capitalism. In both cases, it was a disappointing end to a decade which at one point had promised so much.

But in any event Ireland was, for better or worse, reconnected with the rest of the world, and it was a world wherein many strange things were happening: moon landings,

Asian wars, cultural revolutions, continued student unrest. In terms of rock music, also, 1969 was somewhat of a 'lost' year, with many people from within the fraternity – musicians, management, labels, journalists – searching for a direction after the Summer of Love and the hippy movement's self-immolation. This sense – part wistfulness, part paranoia – of something having come to an end may be clearly discerned on 'Yes, I Need Someone' by Irish psychedelic rockers Eire Apparent.

The band evolved from various beat and showband outfits (Tony and the Telstars, The Skyrockets, Gene and the Gents) playing around Northern Ireland in the early 1960s. An early incarnation (called The People) featured Henry McCullough, another of those guitar aces which Irish rock managed to produce in its first flush (think of Rory Gallagher, Gary Moore and Eric Bell, amongst others). On moving to London to improve their chances (and, no doubt, to escape the deteriorating situation at home), The People met up with ex-Animal Chas Chandler, who booked them under their new moniker to do a North American tour with his greatest protégé, Jimi Hendrix. By this time Eire Apparent's sound had started to lean Zelig-like towards the 'heavy' psychedelic rock forever associated with Hendrix. There was also a substantial West Coast countryish dimension to the music, however – again, something that was very much in the air at the time – making The Byrds, even more than Hendrix, the prevailing

Best Bit: The ascending single-note guitar sequence beginning at 2.44 – the sound of Jimi spiralling towards the great gig in the sky.

influence on Eire Apparent's recordings. In 1968, perhaps sensing the limited currency of the band's undoubtedly derivative style, McCullough moved on, first to a short (and still somewhat intriguing) stint with folk-trad outfit Sweeney's Men, then to more lucrative gigs with Joe Cocker's Grease Band and later (and most famously) with Paul McCartney's Wings.

Stable-mate Hendrix offered to perform on and produce Eire Apparent's first (and as it turned out, only) album – we know this because he left his name on the cover and his musical fingerprints all over the record. (It also featured contributions from such luminaries as Noel Redding and Robert Wyatt.) Its collection of speaker-hopping, timbre-phasing, feedback-looping, genre-bending songs gives a pretty good impression of where the great man's head was in those final years of his life. Recorded in Los Angeles in October 1968, *Sunrise* was already somewhat dated by the time of its release, for 1967 was the *annus mirabilis* for psychedelic rock (*Surrealistic Pillow* by Jefferson Airplane, *Are You*

Experienced? and *Axis: Bold as Love* by The Jimi Hendrix Experience, *The Doors, Younger than Yesterday* by The Byrds). As a musical document, however, this album nonetheless affords a remarkable insight into the late hippy period and the psychedelic rock which was its defining sound.

Both The Byrds and Hendrix loom large on 'Yes, I Need Someone', which was the album's opening cut as well as the B-side of Eire Apparent's second single. The scene is set right from the off with shrieking feedback jumping from channel to channel, before an acoustic guitar enters playing variations on the brooding E minor that will dominate for the remainder of the song. The whole band kicks in after 16 seconds, and while Davy Lutton's drumming attempts to drive the song forward, Hendrix plays spooky atmospherics around Mike Cox's descending guitar figure. The verse stutters forward on a syncopated beat before the chorus relieves us with a return to a straightforward 4/4 time signature. But it seems that every time that beat is reintroduced, it's held up again by hesitations and uncertainties, as if the time signature itself is being haunted by the musical complexities it has temporarily displaced and which it contains within itself.

The musical vacillation of 'Yes, I Need Someone' reflects a lyric that is all about indecision, and the feelings of powerlessness and paranoia that accompany it. 'Yes, I need someone' sounds like a positive statement, but it's mitigated later in the phrase by the words 'to help me make my mind up'. This protagonist isn't certain at all, isn't sure of anything; the song's persistent monochord may give the impression of a sort of muscular wilfulness, but it is in fact underpinned by the vulnerability and self-doubt that follow from having 'been hurt so many times'. The drugs, we may assume, weren't working like they used to.

Taken in its entirety, 'Yes, I Need Someone' is a distillation of two years of acid-fuelled rock experimentation. Besides the music, the reference to 'my mind' and its troubles serves to date and locate it pretty precisely to late-1960s West Coast America. Alienated and suspicious on the one hand, exposed and needy on the other, this was the sound of the inauspicious autumn that followed the golden summer. By the time Eire Apparent returned to Britain in early 1969, the scene had moved on. So, indeed, had their home country. The band broke up in May 1970 and individual members turned to a range of other projects with varying degrees of success.

Sign on My Mind

DR STRANGELY STRANGE [VERTIGO]

The 1960s swung into history, and the new decade opened with roughly equal measures of confusion and confidence. The previous year's Woodstock festival had been the culmination of a decade's counter-cultural activity, but it left many people feeling restless and somehow unfulfilled. What now? With the 1960s done and dusted, where was the energy, the idealism, the radicalism to go? In many ways, in fact, 1970 was a transitional year. In Vietnam, the war dragged on, but human feet had (so they say) walked on the moon just a few months earlier. The Beatles officially announced the end of the party, while Simon and Garfunkel's magisterial *Bridge Over Troubled Water* extended pop's remit to previously unimagined areas.

In Ireland, the 1960s had been a decade of change and relative prosperity, with the sweeping away of many of the attitudes left over from the Civil War, and the opening up to international influences. But civil unrest in Northern Ireland and the fragility of the economic recovery were indications of the way things might (and eventually did) turn.

The showbands were still doing pretty good business, but it was clear to many that a sea-change had overtaken popular music in Ireland. A rock sensibility – the idea of composing, recording and performing original music as a means of self-expression – had imprinted itself upon the island's youth, and was beginning to exert serious influence over the island's entertainment and leisure trends. The showbands wouldn't go away (they still haven't) but they couldn't hope to retain the pre-eminence that they had enjoyed during the glory days of the 1960s. Covers of clichéd love songs and novelty numbers by besuited glamour boys just weren't cutting it for the country's youth any longer. Popular music was becoming more eclectic and more diverse, with many musicians realizing that they could combine the onus to entertain with what they considered to be an equally pressing need to express ideas, beliefs and emotions in musical form.

It's in this transitional context that we can locate a three-piece, Dublin-based band playing a kind of music that mixed elements from the folk, psychedelic, medieval and blues traditions. Ivan Pawle (an Englishman), Tim Booth and Tim Goulding met in the mid 1960s as members of Dublin's burgeoning rock music community. Though studying at Trinity College in their spare time, the trio's consuming passion was music. All multi-instrumentalists and songwriters, their music was influenced in part by the folk boom emerging from the US and the UK and in part by the lifestyle and political principles of the hippy movement. After playing the flourishing folk circuit around Dublin in various combinations, Pawle, Booth and Goulding came together to form the nucleus of Dr Strangely Strange.

Interesting times. Despite their educated, middle-class backgrounds, these 'gownies' hung out in Mount Street and Sandymount flats with working-class 'townies' like Brush Shiels and Philip Lynott. They entertained Mike Heron and Robin Williamson of Scottish group The Incredible String Band, with whom the Strangelys became closely linked owing to the ostensible similarity in sound and outlook (the influence is undeniable). Their Sunday afternoon gigs in Slattery's of Capel Street were legendary laid-back affairs, with various friends – folkies, rockers, traditionalists – sitting in for extended jams. If, in terms of professionalism and ethos, Dr Strangely Strange were some way removed from Van Morrison singing 'Caravan' over in Woodstock, then they were a universe away from Dickie Rock crooning 'Come Back to Stay' in the ballrooms of romance. In fact, it would probably be fair to say that Dr Strangely Strange were 'amateurish', but in all the positive senses of that word: enthusiastic, open-minded, less worried about the audience than the music, and concerned above all to say something meaningful about the world in which they found themselves.

The band recorded their first album, *Kip of the Serenes*, in London in 1969 for Island Records, at that time a small independent label just beginning to get involved with progressive folk. The album was made in less than two days, and consisted of ten original songs performed by the three members on a variety of predominantly acoustic

....

Best Bit: The beginning of the guitar solo proper at 4.12, the subtlety and thoughtfulness of which belies the idea of Moore as nothing more than an effects-laden speed king.

....

instruments. Many of the characteristics of the band's sound are apparent in the first track, 'Strangely Strange (but Oddly Normal)' – key and tempo changes, code-mixing, nursery-rhyme lyrics which offer themselves for interpretation on a number of levels. The stand-out track is Booth's 'Donnybrook Fair'. After a pavan-like introduction, the lyric invokes Ireland's famous medieval carnival as a place where the unicorn (apparently representing freedom from restraint and tradition) is symbolically ranged alongside and against a number of venerable historical figures (including Joseph Mary Plunkett and Pádraic Pearse – serious stuff, only four years after the triumphalist celebrations of the Easter Rising's fiftieth anniversary). 'Oh, it is possible to do anything,' the singer warbles, more in wishful thinking, one suspects, than as a reflection of contemporary Irish reality.

The band's second album was a more expansive affair, with the recruitment of various friends contributing to a rockier, less eccentric sound. 'Sign on My Mind' is the outstanding cut from *Heavy Petting* (1970) – 8 minutes and 45 seconds that communicate more about the late hippy period than volumes of scholarly analysis ever could.

Ivan Pawle sings his own composition in that fey, delicate and peculiarly 'English' voice typical of the hippy end of the British folk revival. (Williamson, Heron and Donovan offered Scottish variants, but the style is best represented in the impossibly delicate strains of legendary English prog folkie, Nick Drake.) The lyric, also, concerns one of the favourite post-*Pepper* hippy themes: perception, its possibilities and, more insistently, its limitations. If the doors of perception had been prised open in the early part of the 1960s, events in places like Memphis and Altamont, Paris and Prague (not to mention Belfast) had conspired to slam them shut again. 'Things aren't what they would appear,' laments Pawle, and the music agrees. The song longs for resolution in its home key of D, but keeps getting drawn back into a wistful, weary Em–F#m progression. On first hearing, you get the impression that the extended penny whistle solo after the first chorus should stand as the musical equivalent of the downbeat lyric; it is, after all, what the listener would have been used to in a Strangely Strange song up to that point. As things turn out, however, the whistle merely functions as a prelude to the track's true tragic voice, Gary Moore's weeping guitar solo. Lasting over 3 minutes and growing in complexity with each passing bar, Moore's precocious contribution (he had only just turned eighteen) perfectly complements the mood of regret and melancholy created by Pawle's lyric and the band's plaintive ensemble performance.

'Sign on My Mind' stands as a fitting valediction to a decade of awakening and promise: it's been a blast, the song seems to say, but now we have to come down, and that's always an odd trip, confused and nostalgic by turns. As a description of *Heavy Petting* as a whole, in fact, one could do worse than 'confused and nostalgic'. Dr Strangely Strange broke up in late 1970, although the individual members of the band continued to pop up from time to time in later years in various guises and combinations. Their first two albums, however, testify to the existence of a fiercely creative and highly intelligent sensibility at large in Ireland at the dawn of the 1970s.

1971

Night of the Warm Witch

SKID ROW [CBS]

Nineteen-seventy-one was a vintage year for 'progressive rock', the genre which in many respects took over from psychedelia. The list of seminal releases from that year includes *The Yes Album, Alpha Centauri* by Tangerine Dream, *Tarkus* by Emerson, Lake and Palmer, *From the Witchwood* by The Strawbs, *At Fillmore East* by The Allman Brothers Band, *Monster Movie* by Can, *Meddle* by Pink Floyd, *Nursery Cryme* by Genesis, *Led Zeppelin IV, The Low Spark of the High Heeled Boys* by Traffic and *Islands* by King Crimson. To this list should be added *34 Hours,* the second long-player from Irish trio Skid Row, comprising Brendan 'Brush' Shiels (bass, vocals), Gary Moore (guitar) and Noel 'Nollaig' Bridgeman (drums). The title refers to the amount of studio time it took to record an album which must stand as one of the most frequently referenced, yet least known, of Irish engagements with the international phenomenon of rock music.

Skid Row had been knocking around Dublin in one form or another since 1967. The band either included or were friends with most of the movers and shakers from the contemporary Irish rock scene, including of course Philip Lynott. Still only teenagers by the time they won a contract with CBS in 1969, Skid Row's third, classic format mirrored the three-piece line-up of similar 'progressive' outfits such as Cream and The Jimi Hendrix Experience: kit, bass and killer guitarist. In this format Skid Row toured extensively throughout Europe and the US where they mixed it up with some of the pre-eminent rock names of the day. The band seemed poised for bigger things until, unhappy with both his own role and the direction they were taking, trump card Moore quit just before Christmas 1971.

The moment of Skid Row was *the* moment of 'progressive rock', and their music demonstrates all the hallmarks and all the limitations of that much vilified term. The band's take on the genre seems to have been to combine the guitar-oriented, blues-based virtuosity of Cream with various strands of late 1960s experimental rock, including psychedelia and country. The results weren't always very clear, or indeed very successful, for which we can adduce two related reasons. First of all, you can blame progressive rock itself, which many people (post-punk journalists for the most part) have characterized as simply a victory for inflated style over any kind of substance. Listening to Skid Row now, you occasionally get the impression that musicianship was an end in itself rather than a means to the expression of something else, some non-musical meaning that existed prior to or outwith the music itself.

On the other hand, a dedication to virtuosity, allied with frequently outlandish pomposity, didn't stop any of the other bands mentioned above from producing occasionally memorable music from within the 'progressive' fold. The second point to

Best Bit: Noel Bridgeman's drumming during the extended coda which presents a playful middle finger to the convention of percussive 'accompaniment'.

consider, then, is that although Shiels, Bridgeman and Moore were obviously talented (and in the latter's case, brilliant) musicians, perhaps they simply lacked any vision or ambition other than to play – play anything – together well. Progressive rock was an ostensibly adult-oriented genre that came into being with the maturation of the first white rock 'n' roll generation of the 1960s. These were on the whole older guys who had been through the whole beat and rhythm 'n' blues thing, and who with the fading of the 1960s began to aspire towards the aesthetic values of the established cultural institutions. But there's an unmistakable note of callowness informing the entire Skid Row oeuvre, an impression that despite the high ambition these are merely boys playing at being men. During the band's career they did play, literally, with the big boys (The Allman Brothers Band, The Grateful Dead, Fleetwood Mac and so on), but always seemed to lack the extra-musical experience – the life stuff – to ground their undoubted musical maturity.

These limitations aside, however, Skid Row still represent a hugely significant moment in the evolution of Irish rock, not for the (limited) international success they achieved nor for the uncertain quality of the music they produced, but for the seriousness with which they undertook their musical mission. The phrase 'into the music' might have been coined just for them. Claiming the legacy of international rock as their natural

1971

birthright, the three band members – indeed, all the extended Skid Row family – not only broadened the cultural horizons of all subsequent Irish popular musicians, but also helped to consolidate popular music as the pre-eminent leisure pursuit of the majority of the island's youth generation, then and since. No small achievement for lads for whom shaving was a relatively new experience.

Clocking in at just over 9 minutes, 'Night of the Warm Witch' represents an obvious challenge to the dominant conventions of the 3-minute pop song. It's also an indication of how far serious rock music had 'progressed' in the few short years since the first experimental moves were made by British and American rock musicians. Highly complex in form, arcane in theme, this was a self-elected serious music deliberately at odds with the mainstream generic descendents of rock 'n' roll.

'Night of the Warm Witch' is literally more than just a 'song', moreover, as it comes with its own overture and coda. The song proper is prefaced by a 1-minute introduction, which itself is broken into two parts: 30 seconds of double-tracked guitar (one playing chords through a wah-wah pedal, the other picking out an obscure melody using a difficult technique – sometimes known as 'violining' – in which the little finger of the right hand adjusts volume control as the string is played by a plectrum or another finger) played over a repeated bass figure, followed by 30 seconds of disjointed, distorted electric guitar. The 'coda', meanwhile, begins at 7.30, just as the 'real' song – with its verses and choruses and musical hooks – finishes, and comprises over ninety seconds of unstructured 'jamming' between the four main instruments. No 'fade out' here, no Rory-style closure in which the final chord is prolonged with drum rolls and scalar improvisations until, after a pause and nod from the musical leader, the whole band crashes out of the song. Instead, we have bass, kit and double-tracked guitars improvising their way out of the main musical structure towards a place in which the music, rather than 'ending', is abandoned.

Amongst other things, then, the coda to 'Night of the Warm Witch' represents the defeat of institutionally sponsored notions of 'music', even quite trendy and successful ones, by a much more 'mature' conception of 'noise'. If we're a long way from David Cassidy on the one hand, we're not much nearer The Rolling Stones on the other. The technique of framing and fragmenting a 'song' in this manner was borrowed from avant-gardist art music and contemporary jazz practices, and was typical of progressive rock's desire to challenge normative popular-music practices. The listening experience was both more active and more demanding than that required by 'ordinary' popular music in any of its contemporary forms. Whether the result is worth the effort remains, of course, open to debate.

Silver Song

MELLOW CANDLE [DERAM]

The great Irish historian Roy Foster chose to end his monumental history of modern Ireland in 1972. He did this to signal that the year in question represented a watershed in many ways for the island. On 22 January the Republic signed a treaty of accession to the European Economic Community (one of the forerunners of the European Union) which would become effective on the first day of the following year. Just over a week later, on 30 January, there occurred the events in Derry which history came to know as 'Bloody Sunday'. In March, the Northern Irish Government was suspended by the British Secretary of State, William Whitelaw, to be replaced by direct rule from Westminster. And in December, the citizens of the Republic chose (by referendum) to remove mention of the Catholic Church's 'special position' from the constitution.

These were all fairly significant events in the struggle between modernization and tradition which many perceive to be the animating crisis of modern Irish history (and which, in one form or another, continues to set the socio-cultural and politico-economic agenda down to the present day). Another historian (Terence Brown of Trinity College, Dublin) notes a lower-profile but perhaps ultimately more significant event from 1972: a report from the Commission on the Status of Women noting the failure of the southern state to meet the expectations (or, indeed, the legal requirements) of its female citizens. Fifty years after independence, Irish women were still grossly under-represented in island life; when they did manage to put in an appearance, they were invariably subject to a range of debilitating stereotypes. This was as true of popular music as it was of any other modern Irish sphere – more so, in fact, because despite its self-proclaimed recalcitrance *vis-à-vis* 'straight' society, few cultural practices in the opening years of the 1970s were as conservative as rock music when it came to gender relations.

All these issues were brought together in a mixed-sex, five-piece Dublin band called Mellow Candle, who in 1972 released a brilliant, beautiful collection entitled *Swaddling Songs* – generally agreed (at least by those aware of its existence) to be one of the most affecting and most effective popular-musical documents of its era. The band comprised Clodagh Simmonds (keyboard, vocals), Alison O'Donnell (vocals), David Williams (guitar), Frank Boylan (bass) and Willie Murray (drums). As teenagers, the two women had already experienced 'swinging London' when they recorded a one-off record there in the mid 1960s. Back in Dublin they partook of a musical melting pot (associated in particular with the Lizzy/Strangely 'Orphanage') comprising folk, trad, rock and various related styles. In 1968, Simmonds and O'Donnell teamed up with the lads to play a number of showcase gigs around the capital; their live debut was as support to The Chieftains in Liberty Hall, but they also shared bills with Tír Na nÓg, Thin Lizzy and Skid Row. Having signed with Deram in April, the band relocated to London in December 1971 under the management of Lizzy's Ted Carroll. There they recorded and released, to general public apathy, their only original album (a collection of out-takes and unreleased material entitled *The Virgin Prophet* would appear in the 1990s) before changing their name, splitting and moving on to different projects.

Nineteen-seventy-two was an inauspicious year for sensitive folk-rock from the provinces. In that very year, in fact, rock was in the process of being upstaged by its pop alter ego. The world witnessed the emergence of a new generation of teen idols in the shape of Donny Osmond, David Cassidy, Michael Jackson and Gilbert O'Sullivan (the latter an emigrant Irish singer-songwriter whose crafted tunesmithery belied his pop status). Sweat (*à la* the blues family) and perceptiveness (*à la* folk) were out of fashion; glamour was the order of the day. Some of the platform-balancing, glitter-soaked, make-up-caked British pop acts who broke big that year included Gary Glitter, Marc Bolan, Wizzard, Sweet and Slade. The 'glam' movement – and the attitudes it encompassed – was encapsulated, however, by two releases from June: the eponymous first album by Roxy Music and *The Rise and Fall of Ziggy Stardust and the Spiders from Mars* by David Bowie. The

Best Bit: The entry of the second voice halfway through each verse, subtly shifting the meaning of the song (whatever it may be) from affirmative unison to weaving, ambiguous harmony.

latter was an era-defining and, as it turns out, enduringly influential reflection on the figure of the modern 'pop star' at a crucial stage of its development.

Half a world away from the pouting and parading of the glam bands existed the curiosity that was British folk rock. An unstable marriage of the folk boom of the early 1960s and the hippy counter-culture of the later part of the decade, folk rock nevertheless represents one of the most original responses to the rock 'n' roll revolution to have emerged from the old world. The leading representatives of the genre tended to share a number of characteristics: a folk diva (for example, Jacqui McShee, Sandy Denny and Maddy Prior, of Pentangle, Fairport Convention and Steeleye Span respectively) backed by male instrumentalists of various persuasions, though usually featuring a killer guitarist such as Bert Jansch, John Renbourn, Richard Thompson or Martin Carthy. (The Irish husband-and-wife team of Gay and Terry Woods had formed part of the original Steeleye Span line-up and contributed significantly to the band's seminal debut, *Hark! The Village Wait,* from June 1970.) Some of these bands were 'folkier' than others; some incorporated elements of jazz, blues and other rootsy styles into their sound. All pushed the envelope, however, regarding the mixture of 'folk' and 'rock' (the latter, of course, being itself a prodigal descendent of Euro-American folk music).

This is clearly the world to which Mellow Candle belonged (in fact they gigged with both Fairport and Steeleye Span during their time in England) – the world of progressive folk in which the borders between different musical categories, and different perceptions of reality, were constantly tested. Now, it is a fact that the role and representation of women in the world of prog folk (or indeed in its hippy parent movement) has never been properly considered. One thing is certain, however: coming as they did from a culture whose values were significantly different from those in which the genre first developed, the experience of composing and performing music must have impacted differently on Simmonds and O'Donnell than it did on their British counterparts. This difference, moreover, may perhaps be discerned in the music itself.

The only single culled from the album was Simmonds's 'Silver Song' – a record which, like *Swaddling Songs* itself, sank without trace upon its initial release. The song's vague lyrics relate a familiar hippy tale of 'my' emotional and psychic dispossession at 'their' hands, played out against a backcloth of suburban domesticity. The key opposition lies between nature (always a 'good' force in folk discourse, and frequently represented, there as elsewhere, as female) and 'bad' materialism – the (invariably male) tendency to objectify human effort. The music is unsettled and unsettling, beginning with a chromatic descent in Cm before modulating halfway through each verse into Fm. The gaps between vocal lines are filled by tinkly keyboards, brooding strings and a fiddly guitar which recalls Richard Thompson's work on Fairport classics such as 'Who Knows Where the Time Goes?' (1969). Ultimately, however, the music is as nebulous and unresolved as the lyric, refusing to 'name' itself or its relationship with the real world. And it's precisely this reluctant beauty which has made *Swaddling Songs* such a cult classic (and such a collector's item) in the years since its release.

If you think of the protagonist as a young woman, much of the 'meaning' of this song starts to come into focus; if you think of the protagonist as a young *Irish* woman, the song begins to assume dark overtones relating back to a history of marginalization and abuse that is still emerging. Mellow Candle may not have self-consciously engaged with this history in their music, but it *is* there nonetheless. Would 'Mother Ireland' ever be the same again?

The Rocker

THIN LIZZY [DECCA SKL]

Most people who care about such matters tend to regard the Thin Lizzy of *Live and Dangerous* (1978) as the definitive line-up – that is, original Irish members Brian Downey and Philip Lynott on drums and bass, plus guitarists Brian Robertson from Scotland and Scott Gorham from California. They're probably right. Robertson and Gorham joined late in 1974, after the band had used up Eric Bell, Gary Moore, John Cann and Andy Gee. Although the first couple of albums on which they played, *Nightlife* (1974) and *Fighting* (1975), were alright, the developing chemistry between the two wunderkinder contributed significantly to Lizzy's golden period, which included the albums *Jailbreak* (1976), *Johnny the Fox* (1976) and *Bad Reputation* (1977), and culminated in 1978's justly celebrated double live album, *Live and Dangerous*.

The same people also tend to think that Lizzy's success was predicated on the enigmatic 'rocker-romantic' persona developed by Lynott in such songs as the transatlantic hit 'The Boys Are Back in Town' (1976) – in many ways, Lizzy's signature track – and beautifully realized meditations on 'softer' personal issues such as 'Sarah' (1979), 'Old Town' (1982) or 'Little Girl in Bloom' (1973). These songs encapsulate the classic stand-off between the 'tough' and the 'tender' on which rock 'n' roll has relied so heavily since its inception. In this respect, Lynott's contribution to rock's narrative repository was twofold: on the one hand, he helped develop the influential sub-narrative of the 'band-as-gang' which has had such wide currency in the years since Lizzy strutted their stuff; on the other, Philo deliberately cultivated a character in which the 'tough' and the 'tender', the 'rocker' and the 'romantic', vie continuously for dominance. Lynott could do the leather-trousered, macho front man and the sensitive, reflective poet equally well, although he eventually had to dissociate the two by developing a solo career. A large part of Thin Lizzy's contemporary success, however, as well as the band's subsequent place in rock history, depended in large part on the complex interplay between the two archetypes.

Specific songs may be identified as emerging from one or other of Lynott's fictional personas, but occasionally the affiliations are more subtle. In 'The Boys Are Back in Town', for example, the narrator inscribes the classic 'Beat' values – most fully articulated in Jack Kerouac's *On The Road* (1957) – which had such a profound influence on American rock music: freedom, friendship and fucking (the romantic) on the one hand, disaffection, violence and misogyny (the rocker) on the other. At the same time, the music itself embodies this ambiguity, with the power chords (representing the latter set of values) vying for dominance with Gorham's more nuanced fretwork and the tightly harmonized melodies produced by the twin lead guitars (representing the former) at various points throughout the song, but especially during the fade-out. Philo's vocal style, likewise, was always capable of more expression and subtlety than most of his harder rocking contemporaries. All told, Lizzy's achievement in this great song was to give narrative form to the contradictions upon which rock 'n' roll itself was formulated.

But of course the band had a sizeable recording catalogue well before Robertson and Gorham signed up. After the dust had settled in 1970, Lynott, Downey and Bell came together to form the first significant version of Thin Lizzy. And although his

....

Best Bit: The final, heavily phased A6 chord (2.33), which manages to invoke the pop romance of The Beatles alongside the brooding rock presence of Jimi Hendrix.

....

imagination clearly continued to grow throughout a comparatively long career, it wouldn't be unreasonable to assume that many of the major aspects of Lynott's vision as an artist were already well established by 1973. This being the case, it's interesting that the significant musical and lyrical themes for which the later line-up are best remembered had their basis in that earlier incarnation. This is something that is clearly discernible in 'The Rocker', a song which functions to all intents and purposes as 'The Boys Are Back in Town' Mark I.

'The Rocker' possesses all the aggression of 'Boys', but with little of its mitigating subtlety or romance. Rather than being focalized through an admiring minor participant (as in the later song), the rocker himself addresses us, and this is a somewhat unsettling experience. Here's a guy who welcomes 'trouble', who hangs out 'down at the juke joint' with 'the boys', and whose chief interests are 'dirty jokes' and 'records'. Lynott would no doubt have met many of these types at the Rock On music stall owned and run by Ted Carroll (then manager of Thin Lizzy) in London's Portobello Road during the Teddy Boy revival of the early 1970s. The music is appropriate for such a character, for although far from a blues-rock outfit in the Rory mould, this three-piece Lizzy manage to kick up an impressive storm. Despite some 'psychedelic' guitar after the first bridge (at 1.57), there's no sign of the folk or hippy elements which had characterized the first two albums. Downey and Bell turn in busy but extremely tight performances which perfectly complement one of Philo's most robust vocals. Singing close to the top of his range, he 'plays' the rocker as simultaneously cool and agitated, a dangerous customer whose personality combines two parts menace to one part arrogance.

One thing the two songs do have in common, however, is an ambivalent attitude towards women, and once again this is something which goes to the heart of rock 'n' roll mythology. The 'chick' violently spurned in the first verse ('Hey little girl, keep your hands off me') is actively courted in the second ('Hey baby, meet me, I'm a tough guy, got my cycle outside, you wanna try?'). Her response? 'Ooh, I'd do anything for you, 'cos you're a rocker!' I don't know if the great man had met any of the second-wave feminists – such as Germaine Greer (*The Female Eunuch,* 1970) or Juliet Mitchell (*Women's Estate,* 1971) – whose work was contemporaneous with 'The Rocker'. It's a safe bet, however, that they would have had issues with the model of gender relations deployed in this particular recording.

This is somewhat beside the point, though, for it's clear that 'The Rocker' is making intertextual reference to one of the most resonant icons of post-war American popular culture, specifically the tough-but-sensitive character portrayed by the likes of Marlon Brando in *The Wild One* (1954) and Elvis Presley in *Roustabout* (1964). The temporal and geographical displacement helps to mitigate the track's overt sexism; after all, it's not the Irishman in 1973 who professes these values and sentiments but the character he has 'borrowed' from America's recent past. In that sense, the reconstructed twenty-first-century Philophile can still maintain a positive relationship with tracks like 'The Rocker'.

At the same time, there were more immediate influences available, and we don't have to travel so far to discover resonant variations on both the 'rocker' and the 'romantic' in Irish cultural history. The tough-but-sensitive image which has fuelled the Philo cult in the years since his untimely death emerged as much in response to *that* history – the 'niceness' of the showbands, for example, or the country's ambivalent gender politics, or his own status as both insider and outsider – as it did to the invocation of popular American iconography. And while not wanting to get beyond ourselves, we could say that Thin Lizzy's bequest to rock – a swagger tinged with wistfulness, simultaneous urges to go and to stay – has its basis in a peculiarly Irish cultural dynamic.

1974

Streets of Arklow

VAN MORRISON [POLYDOR]

It's important to bear in mind that Van was already a veteran of the popular music industry by the time he came to write and record *Veedon Fleece* in 1974. Even if he had never stepped into a studio or on to a stage again, the first ten years or so of his career guaranteed him a place in rock history, both in terms of music produced and vision pursued. The journey from fresh-faced showband musician with The Monarchs to rhythm 'n' blues shouter with Them to the mystical rock poet of *Astral Weeks* (1969) traces what is in many ways *the* archetypal rock story: the young white boy migrates from a local, primarily entertainment-oriented popular music, through an identification with more esoteric forms derived from the African-American tradition, and on to deadly serious music-making practices in which personal expression, originality and authenticity are the guiding principles.

Follow-up albums such as *Moondance* (1970) and *St Dominic's Preview* (1972) confirmed the Belfast man as an artist of enduring power and vision. However, those albums were produced at a time when the nascent discourse of rock was confronting for the first time a question which successful artists working in other media had been encountering for centuries: what next? To repeat and consolidate, which in this context meant a return to that entertainment ethos from which self-elected 'genuine' rock artists wished to distance themselves, or to go away and dream it all up again? By 1974, given his relative longevity and success, this was a question that Van, no less than peers like The Rolling Stones or Bob Dylan, had to ask of himself. The beginnings of an answer may be found on *Veedon Fleece*.

On this album we hear the music harking back to the free-form meanderings of *Astral Weeks* after the more tightly structured writing and playing found on the intermediate material. More than that, after the years of American exile, *Veedon Fleece* represented an extended re-engagement with the homeland as a place within the artist's evolving spiritual imagination. The cover, with its green background, Irish wolfhounds and country-park vista, is a bit of a giveaway. And then there's the music. The opening track takes its title from a peculiarly Irish locution ('fair play to ye'), connoting a generally positive response of admiration and encouragement. It would seem that in some ways, Ireland itself – the lakes, architecture, streets and meadows mentioned in the lyric of 'Fair Play' – may be seen as the admired and deserving subject of the song, and of the collection as a whole. Ireland is figured as a place of mystery, imagination and dreams. As the album

unfolds, it's also the imaginary location of an innocent, youthful relationship with nature, a fair country where the singer may leave behind the melancholy feeling which has overtaken him. Just the tonic after divorce and disillusionment had forced Morrison to wake from his American dream. Moreover, what with Tricky Dickie Nixon's infamous resignation, famine in Bangladesh, war in Cyprus and imminent world recession in the wake of the previous year's oil crisis, it's no wonder that the sensitive artist was in need of some serious soul-healing. Similar realizations regarding the onset of major change may be found on other rock releases from both sides of the Atlantic in 1974, including Tim Buckley's *Look at the Fool* and George Harrison's *Dark Horse.*

'Streets of Arklow' is a brooding quasi-ballad in the key of E minor. If the piece has all the folky feelings introduced on *Astral Weeks,* however, it clearly derives from the dark end of the spectrum, retaining enough mystery and menace to make it an unsettling listening experience even thirty years later. The title self-consciously evokes the world

••

Best Bit: The entry of the strings at the beginning of the third verse (2.19), which suddenly give an epic sweep to a world which the song had led us to consider low key and parochial.

••

of Irish balladry, with its allusion to both the sub-genre of the place-name song, and the familiar 'streets of …' convention. Like most folk songs, 'Streets of Arklow' tells a story; *unlike* most folk songs, however, it doesn't tell you what the story is. If that sounds paradoxical, it's because, typically of Morrison's method, the piece works more by suggestion and atmosphere than by the building up of a coherent set of images and details. This itself may be put down to the artist's vision and technique, which throughout his career has been concerned with the immanence of the extraordinary within the everyday, and the survival of the mystical alongside the material. At times, it seems, the relationship between Ireland and the rest of the world functions for Morrison as an allegory of this vision, something which must have been on his mind as he prepared to forsake the bright lights of Los Angeles and New York (where the album was recorded) for the murky twilight world of 1970s Ireland.

The acoustic guitar with which 'Streets of Arklow' opens is soon joined by bass, drums and a bluesy piano. The gloominess is temporarily relieved by a modulation to C, at which point the vocal also enters. Immediately we sense the kind of world to which we're just about to be introduced: the opening word ('and'), typical of folk and/or fairy narratives, suggests an established, ongoing story, while the 'we' represents a community of protagonists and listeners, something fundamentally opposed to the singular rock persona associated with the classic pop-rock canon in which *I* can't get no satisfaction, *I* wanna hold your hand, *I* was so much older then, and so on.

A flute enters immediately after that first line, and it will continue to trouble the vocal for the duration of the track. Played by American Jim Rothermel, this instrument certainly makes 'Streets of Arklow' *sound* like a traditional Irish song at times, and in that respect it prepares the way for the acoustic folkiness Morrison revisited from time to time in later years, culminating in his 1988 collaboration with The Chieftains on the *Irish Heartbeat* album. The flute's restive meandering throughout the song provides the perfect musical accompaniment for the lyric's depiction of Gypsies roaming through a green land with their impassioned hearts. An image further removed from dreary old Arklow in the 1970s – where, as elsewhere in the country, real Gypsies ('knackers' in the popular appellation) were *personae non gratis* – is hard to imagine. Nevertheless, words and music combine to produce a mood of restlessness and mystery, of the magic that insists within the mundane. The name for this mood, which Van spent so much of his subsequent career exploring, is 'Ireland'.

Out on the Western Plain

RORY GALLAGHER [CHRYSALIS]

By the mid 1970s Rory Gallagher stood (alongside Van and Philip Lynott) as one of the island's few credible rock stars. Indeed, it was probably only Philo who could rival Gallagher in terms of the affection and esteem with which he was – and continues to be – held by Irish rock fans. Wowing audiences across the globe with his late 1960s power trio Taste, the guitarist went on to release an impressive string of solo efforts throughout the 1970s, guaranteeing his position as an Irish rock legend. It was no surprise, then, when *An Post* – the Irish Post Office – included an image of Gallagher (along with Van, Phil and U2) in a set of 2002 postage stamps to commemorate Ireland's popular music culture. Admittedly, this type of institutional state endorsement isn't very rock 'n' roll, but it nevertheless signifies Rory's enduring stature in Irish rock history. What's the story of this shy, self-deprecating boy from the cultural backwater of provincial Ireland? And how did he end up as a leading light of one of the twentieth century's most exciting musical forms?

The Rory story begins with a sort of internal migration, with the Gallagher family leaving the youngster's birthplace in Ballyshannon, Co. Donegal, for the south-western county of Cork, the region with which he would become forever associated. Developing an early fascination for the electric guitar, Rory picked up his first instrument aged nine, before forming his first band at the age of thirteen. Indeed, the guitarist was still attending school when he won his live-performance spurs with local showband The Fontana. Later renamed The Impact, this outfit went on to enjoy a post-Beatles residency slot on Hamburg's famous Reeperbahn, before Rory returned to Cork to form Taste.

By this stage (1966), the British blues revival was in full swing, and Gallagher's reputation quickly spread to the English capital, where his band frequently travelled to support some of the scene's foremost acts, including The Jimi Hendrix Experience and Cream. Taste's material was typical of the mid-1960s blues rock widely associated with the likes of John Mayall's Bluesbreakers, Fleetwood Mac and the aforementioned

Cream. An extraordinarily dynamic (and often highly demanding) style, the emergent sub-genre was a heady fusion of diverse musical origins, including rock 'n' roll, rhythm 'n' blues and jazz.

Quickly establishing himself as one of the form's leading exponents, Gallagher led Taste through a brace of long-players – as well as an extensive touring programme – before performing a show-stealing farewell set at the Isle of Wight Festival in August 1970. Classic singles like 'Blister on the Moon' (1968) and 'Born on the Wrong Side of Time' (1969) had ensured Rory's position in the roll-call – along with Clapton, Page and Green – of great white electric blues guitarists. Indeed, when The Rolling Stones began auditions for a second guitar player in 1974, Gallagher was short-listed as the ideal choice. However, with four impressive solo albums – and the seminal *Live in Europe* collection (1972) – now under his belt, Rory had his own career to consider, and the self-effacing Corkman politely declined. Instead of drug-fuelled jam sessions with Jagger and Richards, then, Rory returned to work on his now celebrated *Irish Tour* album and movie (1974), which offered a brilliant synopsis of the guitarist's early solo efforts ahead of a planned career relaunch with major label Chrysalis. The vast bulk of this solo work had mined a similar blues-rock vein to that of Taste – not least on what would become Rory's de facto signature tune 'Bullfrog Blues' (1972) – but he had also introduced various country, folk and jazz strands to his oeuvre, making room for low-key acoustic numbers in both his studio sets and live performances. On stage, meanwhile, Rory had developed a highly distinctive visual style based around a trademark lumberjack shirt and battered brown Strat. Indeed, it was a close-up shot of the latter that provided the artwork for Gallagher's debut collection for Chrysalis, *Against the Grain* (1975).

Showcasing both the frenzied rock ('Souped-Up Ford') and serene acoustic (Ain't Too Good') sides of the Gallagher aesthetic, the record also offered a nod – via its cover of the Leadbelly classic 'Out on the Western Plain' – to the original sources on which Rory's career had been based. Recounting an archetypal 'cowboy' narrative, this stirring acoustic number unveils an ostentatiously 'macho' persona, with the song's speaker casually boasting about the enormous wealth that he pulled in on the bridle reins, before reflecting coolly on the glorious gunfight he enjoyed with one Jesse James.

The rugged masculinity of the song's persona had scarcely been anticipated by Rory's high-register 'scat' singing in the song's opening bars. However, it was indubitably underscored by the deep, sonorous sounds of the Martin acoustic that Gallagher had set to the non-standard 'folk' tuning known as 'DADGAD' (signifying the six notes to which the individual strings are tuned). Closely associated with the Scottish folk singer-guitarist Bert Jansch (who would occasionally collaborate with Rory on traditional songs), this alternate tuning system bestowed the song with a remarkably compelling (and vaguely 'Celtic') resonant drone.

Freed from the harmonic rigidity of standard tuning, Rory was able to conjure – both lyrically and musically – the limitless expanse of the American West, evoking an imaginary space far beyond the narrow confines of mid-70s Ireland. (Although the passing, in 1975, of Nationalist patriarch Éamon de Valéra had underlined the country's shift from its previously insular cultural era, the Republic now had the highest unemployment rates in western Europe, and the sectarian conflict north of the border had extended its brutal violence to the popular-music scene, with the vicious UVF attack on the Miami Showband). This isn't to say, however, that 'Western Plain' wasn't capable of taking on more local resonances, such as when it was performed on Rory's home turf in West Cork, most notably at the Macroom Rock Festival in 1978. But the topographical space invoked by the song is fundamentally that of the American West, a perennial fascination for generations of Irish rock musicians, as witnessed by the desert ghost towns of U2's *Joshua Tree* (1987) and the Californian sojourns of The Thrills. Such pop-cultural evocations of a mythic American West had their origins, of course, in a peculiarly Irish imagination, having been most famously transposed onto the big screen

Best Bit: The inflated bravado of the song's flashy 'macho' persona – it seems that the old bluesman may have been having a sneaky laugh at the cowboy's expense ...

by Hollywood film-maker John Ford (formerly Sean O'Feeney), whose parents hailed from Ireland's very own 'Wild West' in rural Connemara. Indeed, many of the heroic figures that populated this desolate landscape, including Buffalo Bill (who is also name-checked in the Leadbelly song), were the immediate descendants of Irish immigrants to the US.

It was perhaps not such a stretch, then, for the boy from West Cork to take on the persona of ruthless frontiersman, seizing economic opportunity in this inhospitable terrain. Such material success would fail to translate, however, into Gallagher's own career, for despite Chrysalis's plans to elevate Rory into rock's premier league, *Against the Grain* would signal the beginning of his commercial decline. This slump in form wasn't exactly aided by the emergence of punk, whose preliminary tremors could already be registered in 1975 (with The Sex Pistols making their live debut in London while Patti Smith recorded the seminal *Horses* [1975] in New York). Gallagher's unreconstructed blues rock quickly became, for a new generation of young rock fans, the object of contempt and hostility.

Unlike many other figures from this era, however, Rory's reputation managed to survive the epoch-shifting years of the late 1970s, with post-punk guitar heroes like The Edge, Slash and Johnny Marr all acknowledging his influence. Consequently, when news of Rory's death (from complications following a liver operation) filtered through to the world on 14 June 1995, there was genuine shock and grief, not only amongst his dedicated fans in Ireland, but also amongst the many more who, though perhaps not overly familiar with his music, respected him as a great Irish rock institution.

1976

Trouble
(with a Capital T)

HORSLIPS [MOO]

The 'interest' attending the music produced by Horslips throughout the 1970s tends to detract from one highly pertinent fact: they were a kick-ass band who made great music which spoke to the times in which it was made. Their deficiencies *qua* rock band – the lack of a charismatic frontman, the occasionally soulless vocals – are usually apologized for in academic and journalistic accounts with reference to their 'importance' as an Irish rock band. Here, after all, was a group who undertook the first credible fusion of electric rock and traditional folk, who reclaimed the ballroom circuit from the showbands, who remained based in Ireland when the accepted route was the mail boat to Holyhead and who formed their own label rather than signing on the first dotted line that was thrust under their collective nose. All true, but all rather beside the point if the music wasn't up to it. The thing about Horslips is that the music was most definitely up to it, and that despite the sometimes dubious credentials and motives of the people who say they were good (a bit like Shakespeare in this respect), they were in fact very, very good.

The Horslips story is too well known to rehearse here at any length. Suffice to say that after a bit of shuffling in the early 1970s, five young men came together from various backgrounds with the intention of writing, performing and eventually recording a kind of music that had not been attempted before, in Ireland or elsewhere. Between 1972, when they burst on to the Irish music scene with the sparklingly innovative *Happy to Meet, Sorry to Part*, and 1980, when they decided to call it a day in the face of a dwindling muse, Horslips redefined what an Irish rock music might be. 'Irish rock', incidentally, is a much

more felicitous designation (and much more accurate of Horslips' aspirations) than the 'Celtic rock' label which trailed the band from an early stage. Whatever terminology you care to use, however, the band's achievement was immense and their influence wide and deep. Whenever you hear a diddly-eye fiddle playing over a traditional rock rhythm section, or a plaintive whistle vying for attention with an electric guitar, or lyrics which speak to the Irish historical condition, then the ghost of the 'Slips is in the building. This achievement is all the more impressive in retrospect when you realize that the defining terms of the field in which they were attempting to intervene – 'Irish' and 'rock' – were undergoing massive changes throughout the period in which the band was active.

The Book of Invasions (1976) marked a return to the high-concept project first broached in *The Táin* (1973). With that first brilliantly realized sortie into ancient Irish history – more exciting than Steeleye Span, stronger narratives and images than Yes, more humorous than Genesis, less eccentric than Jethro Tull – Horslips left their competitors in the folk-prog fusion stakes standing. Although the next three collections, *Dancehall Sweethearts* (1974), *The Unfortunate Cup of Tea* (1975) and *Drive the Cold Winter Away* (1975), were uneven, they did prove that Horslips weren't a one-idea band, and that their 'folk' and 'trad' credentials were more than a mere affectation. By 1976, however, with punk bubbling under and the whole idea of a 'serious' rock music just about to go out of fashion, the band realized that they were never going to draw the material benefits that went with mainstream success, and the time had come for the definitive statement on the musical genre that they had patented and brought to ultimate expression.

Some feel that once Horslips had made this realization they should have grasped the 'concept album' nettle with both hands, and gone all out for a double- or even triple-album blockbuster which would have enabled them to give full rein to the material with which they had decided to work. Perhaps; it is in fact a very partial (in both senses) version of *Lebor Gabála Érenn* (an important medieval chronicle of the legendary history of Ireland) that eventually emerged. The desire to represent even selected aspects of that history, and to try to do so within the structure of the three principal categories of the ancient Irish song tradition (*geantraí, goltraí* and *suantraí* – roughly translated as the joyous, lamenting and sleeping strains) in one long-playing vinyl record may seem overly ambitious. But that was the point; *The Book of Invasions* was no *Der Ring des Nibelungen*, and Horslips had no Wagnerian pretensions. Rather, here was a working Irish rock band attempting to create some kind of imaginative space within which the two major forces in their lives – Irish heritage and rock 'n' roll music – could converge and combine. It was a brilliant idea, brilliantly executed.

After the low-key instrumental introduction of 'Daybreak' and 'March into Trouble', 'Trouble (with a Capital T)' sets the tone for the remainder of the *geantraí* section which occupies the whole of side one. It's an odd title, and an odd lyric, when you think about it: presumably neither the Fir Bolg nor their Tuatha de Danann conquerors ever used the word 'trouble' – with or without a capital 't' – when referring to problems encountered in Ireland two and a half millennia ago. But Horslips were not concerned with trying to paint a gloss of 'Celtic' authenticity on their music by deploying some specious heroic language. Rather, the epic imagery ('High on a mountain stands a boat') is set against a level of quotidian experience ('Can't see the fire but we smell the smoke') which attempts to render the *essence* of the narrative. It is in every sense of the word a 'translation' of one world, and the mind-set which sustained it, into another – a sort of dialogue between late-twentieth-century Ireland and one of a number of possible Irelands from the past.

Musically, also, the song offers a model of creative hybridity in the face of cultural change which few subsequent artists have imagined, let alone achieved. The signature riff is played in unison by Johnny Fean and Jim Lockhart on electric guitar and flute, as if to signal the confluence of two musical worlds. That unison is temporarily lost at 1.48 when the key modulates to A, and guitar and flute speak their own truths to each

Best Bit: Barry Devlin's busy bass guitar, which carries the song's complex rhythm while providing a perfect grounding for one of the most memorable of Irish rock riffs.

other in their own peculiar idioms. Not only do key and instrumentation vary over the course of the track, moreover, the steady 4/4 rock beat which drives the riff and the chorus gives way to a 2/4 beat during the verses, changing the emphasis and attack of the music. All told, 'Trouble (with a Capital T)' is a representation *of* a world (ancient Ireland) undergoing change *from* a world (modern Ireland) undergoing its own set of troubles and transformations.

Television Screen

THE RADIATORS FROM SPACE [CHISWICK]

Punk rock had made an explosive entry onto the UK music scene in 1976. Signalling an abrupt break with rock's immediate past, bands like The Sex Pistols and The Clash offered an abrasive, stripped-down riposte to the self-indulgent virtuosity of 1970s supergroups like Led Zeppelin and Pink Floyd. In stark contrast, the new scene's ethos was ferociously DIY, with its leading voices calling for the immediate demystification of rock's phoney 'aura', hence the now famous call to arms in a leading punk fanzine: 'This is a chord. This is another. This is a third. *Now form a band.*'

Cultivating an aesthetic that was markedly lo-fi, early punk groups used fast-tempo rhythms, distorted barre chords and wilfully naive melodies. Vocal styles became especially confrontational, with singers adopting recognizably 'local' accents. Musically, the UK scene was heavily shaped by developments in the US – most notably The Ramones' eponymous debut album (1976), but also American proto-punks like MC5, The Stooges and The New York Dolls. Politically, however, English punks were far more dissenting than their US counterparts, developing a peculiar knack for the insulting gesture, whether it be 'gobbing' on stage, swearing on TV or sporting the swastika as fashion accessory.

At the forefront of the London scene was The Sex Pistols, who produced 1977's definitive punk anthem, 'God Save the Queen'. The Pistols were fronted by 'Johnny Rotten' – actually a second-generation Irish boy named John Lydon whose parents had left their native shore in the 1950s, thereby unwittingly denying the country of one of punk's most distinctive voices. In Ireland itself, though, local punks were beginning to create shockwaves of their own, with the visit of The Clash providing a watershed moment that, for Ballymun teenager Paul Hewson (later U2's Bono), was 'like the cultural revolution'.

Social conditions in the Republic were admittedly less severe than in post-war London (with its high unemployment, industrial unrest and increasing racism), but Irish youth had a right to feel similarly disaffected. Certainly, the mass emigration of the 1950s and 1960s was beginning to slow down, but employment prospects remained scarce, and Catholic conservatism meant the absence – until the late 1970s – of any institutional rock media. (*Hot Press* and 2FM weren't launched until 1977 and 1979 respectively.) The increasing sectarianism of the north, meanwhile, had taken an especially vicious turn, spilling over into the Republic for 1974's O'Connell Street bombing.

From a specifically musical perspective, the country also had its fair share of rock dinosaurs. In truth, the younger generation of musicians probably had some respect for acts like Rory, Van and Horslips, but they were precisely the kind of rock auteurs – trading in 'old school' virtuosity – that punk had set as its targets. There was also – let us not forget – the showbands, ceilidhs and bluesy pub sessions, all of which cast a long shadow over 1970s music. The conditions were therefore ripe for an Irish punk intervention. Enter The Radiators From Space, a group of middle-class art-school boys from Dublin, now widely acknowledged as Ireland's first punk band.

The group had actually begun life in the early part of the 1970s as a glam-rock outfit, Greta Garbage And The Trash Cans, led by Stephen Rapid (vocals) and Pete Holidai (guitar, vocals). Later joined by Philip Chevron (guitar, vocals), Mark Megaray (bass) and James Crash (drums), the band had a brief spell as Bent Fairy And The Punks, before settling on the suitably outlandish Radiators From Space.

After providing local support for the visiting Eddie And The Hot Rods at University College Dublin in November 1976, the band were recommended (by Horslips drummer Eamonn Carr) to Chiswick Records boss Ted Carroll. Shortly thereafter, the group struck a deal with Chiswick, and began work on their debut album, *TV Tube Heart* (1977).

Best Bit: The memorable opening riff, furnishing the track with its most colourful moment.

The record's lead-off single, 'Television Screen', is a rapid-fire blast of a song, coming in at just under 1 minute and 50 seconds. Heralded by Chevron's bright, two-note guitar motif, its musical primitivism was typical of early punk, utilizing a rudimentary twelve-bar blues figure (A–D–E), from which it refuses to deviate.

The track's thrashy three-chord trick was described by the band as an 'amphetamined' take on Chuck Berry's 'Johnny B. Goode' (1958). However, while other punk bands managed to revive 1950s rock 'n' roll motifs beyond the point of recognition (as with The Pistols' sped-up and fuzz-boxed Eddie Cochrane riffs), 'Television Screen''s guitar boogie veers precariously close to the unreconstructed white-boy blues of rock behemoth Status Quo.

What the song lacks in musical invention, though, it makes up for with sheer exuberance. Indeed, its relentless speed, combined with wilfully 'poor' production and anti-virtuoso playing (check out the mangled rhythm 'n' blues guitar solo at 1.06–1.20), bestow the track with unmistakably punk credentials. Meanwhile, Rapid's appropriately speedy – and aggressively unmelodic – vocal delivery connotes rage to the point of inarticulacy, with many of his lyrics being rendered incomprehensible.

In contrast to English punk's highly targeted selection of authoritarian enemies – such as the monarchy ('God Save the Queen'), the police ('White Riot') or the major record labels ('EMI') – Ireland's first punk single sets itself up against a much more generic form of establishment: the 'man in a shiny suit' who moves kids 'off the street and into the schools', the mass media ('network news') and rock dinosaurs ('the rock and roll heroes with the rich man's blues').

Fuelled by adolescent rage ('he could never understand what's going on in my head'), and shortage of cash ('I never see more than a tenner a week'), the song acts as a kind of revenge fantasy against 'the man' ('I'm gonna get him tonight / And teach him a lesson alright'). This sets up the track's memorable chorus, in which an electric guitar becomes the means by which Rapid can finally unleash his angst: 'I'm gonna put a Telecaster through the television screen / 'Cos I don't like what's going on.'

Ultimately a standard punk expression of hostile negation, 'Television Screen' heightened the profile of Dublin's nascent punk scene, with the single reaching a respectable No. 17 in the Irish charts. However, it met with a much less welcoming response in London, the hub of the punk subculture. In the now defunct *Sounds* music paper, for example, the single was cast aside in terms of age-old anti-Irish prejudice: 'Irish punks? Will it start "One, tree, faw, two"?'

Events closer to home were also having a disruptive effect on the band's progress. During a summer punk festival at UCD, an audience member was attacked and fatally stabbed. As the festival's headlining act, The Radiators From Space became public scapegoats, and it soon became difficult for them to book rehearsal space, let alone hire a live venue. After a performance with Thin Lizzy at Dublin's Dalymount Park in August, the band decided to relocate to London, shortening their name to The Radiators in the process. Although they secured a high-profile support slot on Lizzy's UK tour (Philo was a famous friend of punk), the group failed to settle in England, and were soon eclipsed by rival Dublin New Wavers The Boomtown Rats, whose debut single, 'Looking After Number One' (1977), had made the UK Top Twenty.

A second collection of songs – the Tony Visconti-produced *Ghostown* (1979) – was critically well received, but it failed to impress the fans, and by 1981 the group had disbanded. Chevron later experienced success with The Pogues, while Rapid (who had left the group in 1977) became a design consultant for U2. Their belated success was typical of Irish punk, an apparently transitory phenomenon that actually had a profound effect on the country's subsequent rock scene.

Rat Trap

THE BOOMTOWN RATS [ENSIGN]

Like their contemporaries Thin Lizzy and U2, The Boomtown Rats are amongst the most important names in Irish rock history, not only for the quality and the interest of the music they produced, but also because (again like Lizzy and U2) they expanded the boundaries of what Irish popular music could be about. The Rats signed an impressive deal with British label Ensign in February 1977, quite a feat at the time for a non-UK act with only a few dodgy demos to their name (but not untypical of the A&R frenzy that characterized the early months of that year). It should also be recalled that the success of The Boomtown Rats was achieved against major competition from other groups (most of them British and better fancied) who had jumped on the punk bandwagon.

In fact, the Rats were initially portrayed as a punk band, but both their genealogy and their aspirations meant that they always functioned at some distance from the punk ideal. The group's eponymous debut album, and the singles culled from it (including 'Looking After Number One' and 'Mary of the Fourth Form') were unmistakably of punk's first spring – angry, aggressive, raw and uncouth. Bob Geldof, the band's charismatic vocalist and main songwriter, possessed more mouth (if less menace) than a front man like Johnny Rotten; as a former journalist, he also seems to have been attuned to the role of publicity in the popular-music industry from an early stage. In any event, these six young Irish men may have possessed the look and feel of punk, but they had far too much talent (and nous) to be restricted by its performance or lifestyle demands. Of the two bands they supported on British tours in 1977 – The Ramones and Talking Heads – it was towards the rock intelligence of the latter rather than the pop instincts of the former that the Rats gravitated in the period leading up to the release of their second long-player, *A Tonic for the Troops,* in July 1978.

It's fair to say that by the time that record appeared the first cohort of punk rockers had graduated. The Stranglers were still pretty nasty on *Black and White* in May, but their punk credentials had been suspect from the start – they would have been nasty in any era. Rotten had reverted to Lydon after the glorious *Never Mind the Bollocks* (1977) and the decidedly inglorious tour that ensued. The Clash had a quiet summer before releasing *Give 'Em Enough Rope* in November, an album which included the ironic 'All the Young Punks'. The Damned split in February, only to re-emerge in fully-fledged cabaret mode again in the autumn. A generation of performers began to surface which, while taking much of their energy and ethos from punk, blended these with the pop and

rock sensibilities of previous eras. In this respect, it's significant that performers of the calibre of Elvis Costello, The Jam, XTC, The Police, Talking Heads and Blondie all made significant releases during 1978.

It's in the context of these 'New Wave' artists, rather than the earlier pioneers of the punk movement, that the music of The Boomtown Rats should be located. Certainly, many of the attitudes and postures of the latter were profoundly influenced by punk; however, the death of Sid Vicious in February 1979, and the shambles into which the Pistols rump had fallen, were salutary reminders that attitude and posture were nothing without growth and imagination.

For an album peopled with psychos and losers of all kinds, *A Tonic for the Troops* sounds remarkably upbeat. It's as if these time obsessives, social misfits, crazed dictators, recluses and hypochondriacs have decided to hold a party to celebrate their dysfunctionalism. Major keys, rich imagery and bright Beach Boy harmonies lighten even the bleakest of scenarios, as when, for example, the suicides of 'Living in an Island' go to their deaths to the sound of a Caribbean steel band. As a writer, Geldof was no David Byrne, but many of their lyrics approach a similar mood in which terror tinged with a kind of weird

Best Bit: Geldof spits out 'There's gonna be a fight' (1.01), encapsulating the atmosphere of excitement and menace of a summer Saturday night in Anytown.

comedy are depicted as the prevailing conditions of the modern world. Indeed, it was that peculiar combination of surreal paranoia which infused perhaps the Rats' greatest moment, their 1979 hit 'I Don't Like Mondays'.

'Rat Trap' was the stand-out track on *A Tonic for the Troops*. It was a sort of New Wave rewriting of 'Joey's on the Street Again', a rather pedestrian track from the band's first album. As a piece of music, it has more in common with opera than with the traditional 3-minute pop song. Drawing on narrative traditions of kitchen-sink drama, teen movies and urban alienation, 'Rat Trap' tells the story of a brother and sister, Billy and Judy, caught in a cycle of endemic urban poverty and violence. Despite this, the track starts rather jovially in the rousing key of G Major, and introduces a sax motif (unusual in the guitar-dominated punk-pop climate of the time) which will evolve into a fully-fledged solo later on. The famous 'Five Lamps' image at the end of the first verse appears to point to a Dublin location, although this rather misses the point as it's clear that the song is intended to speak to alienated youth everywhere. Both lyrically and musically, in fact, 'Rat Trap' is extremely complex, far removed in both conception and execution from the three-chord, DIY values of the previous summer. Over a quarter of a century later, the self-referential *Top of the Pops* allusion towards the end of the song still has the pop semioticians drooling.

'Rat Trap' remains a landmark in Irish popular-music history in as much as it was the first song by an Irish pop group to get to the top of the British charts. Seeing the band in this oh-so-familiar context – with Geldof cheekily ripping up a photograph of John Travolta (whose *Grease* duet with Olivia Newton John the Rats had displaced at No. 1) – opened the eyes and ears of many Irish people. Sure, Rory was respected, Van was a 'serious' artist, Philo was a 'complex' rocker-romantic, but here was an Irish band playing cutting-edge pop, absolutely assured of their right to success long before Celtic was cool. The theorists may continue to deliberate, but for those who remember that first chart-topping performance there can be no doubt about the connection between popular-music success and national cultural confidence.

Johnny Was

STIFF LITTLE FINGERS [ROUGH TRADE]

By the final year of the decade a relatively vibrant punk scene had built up in Dublin around bands like The Radiators From Space, DC Nein and The Vipers. The city even staged a major punk festival at the Project Arts Centre, a 24-hour event compered by BBC DJ John Peel and featuring bands like The Atrix, The Virgin Prunes and the fledgling U2. Meanwhile, a locally produced compilation album, *Just For Kicks* (1979), served as a vinyl showcase of the city's burgeoning scene. Despite such high-profile interventions, though, the island's best-known engagements with punk undoubtedly took place north of the border. In Belfast, for example, bands like Rudi, Protex and The Outcasts had all released classic punk singles by the end of 1978, while Derry's Undertones had produced one of the genre's canonical tunes in 'Teenage Kicks' (1978).

Easily the best known of the Belfast bands, though, was Stiff Little Fingers, who had begun life as a jobbing pub-rock covers act called Highway Star (a name taken, tellingly, from a Deep Purple song). After the legendary visit of The Clash to Belfast in 1977, the band (led by vocalist/guitarist Jake Burns) swiftly remodelled themselves as a punk outfit, taking their new moniker from a song by London punk band The Vibrators. Despite punk's ideology of self-expression, though, the band – in a curious echo of the showband ethos – assembled their early live sets around faithful renditions of punk standards.

One such show was witnessed by a visiting English journalist named Gordon Ogilvie, who at the time was Ulster correspondent for London's *Daily Express*. He approached Burns and the other band members – Henry Cluney (guitar), Ali McMordie (bass) and Brian Faloon (drums) – suggesting they develop original material based on life in Northern Ireland. For his part, Ogilvie took on managerial responsibilities whilst co-authoring the group's lyrics (a collaboration that would inevitably lead – in the face of punk's 'for real' rhetoric – to accusations of inauthenticity).

The first product of this rather unlikely press-pop partnership was the high-octane agit-punk of 'Suspect Device' (1978), originally released on the group's own Rigid Digits label (before being licensed out to London indie Rough Trade). Evoking the feelings and experiences of alienated youth in late 1970s Belfast, the track – like much of SLF's subsequent output – expressed breathless exasperation at the apparent futility of the Troubles, whilst ferociously renouncing paramilitaries of all hues.

Stylistically, the group's material owed more than a passing debt to the first generation of London punk bands, but they had a distinctive trademark in Burns's rasping bark, which sounded, as one critic famously put it, 'like the frog in his throat died slamming itself against sandpaper'. Moreover, the now instantly recognizable guitar motif that heralded the group's anthemic second single, 'Alternative Ulster' (1978), signalled an immediate punk classic. It was undoubtedly in the live arena, though, that SLF really flourished, with the band gaining a well-earned reputation as a highly visceral live act, capable of attracting 'mixed' (Catholic and Protestant) audiences at their Belfast gigs.

The goal of SLF's debut album was to recreate this live experience in the studio. Recorded in the cellar of a terraced house in Cambridge, England – and co-produced by Rough Trade impresario Geoff Travis – *Inflammable Material* (1979) bore all the hallmarks of punk primitivism. Nevertheless, it proved extremely popular with record-buyers, reaching No. 14 in the UK chart on 21 February 1979 (Burns's twenty-first birthday), and becoming in the process the first indie long-player to break the British Top Twenty.

Taking the situation in Northern Ireland as its unifying theme, the record's stand-out tracks were undoubtedly its two lead-off singles, 'Suspect Device' and 'Alternative Ulster'. While the bulk of the album remained on similar sonic terrain ('Wasted Life', 'White Noise', 'Breakout'), the band occasionally ventured beyond the narrow constraints of the 'straight' punk paradigm, not least in the ironic 'doo wop' middle eight of 'Barbed Wire Love' and the throwaway art-rock of 'Closed Groove'. Most notable in this regard, however, was their radical reworking of 'Johnny Was', Rita Marley's soulful lament on the malign consequences of political violence, originally recorded by Bob Marley and the Wailers.

Clocking in at an unfashionably long 8 minutes, the band cook up an angular – if unashamedly ragged – interpretation of Marley's smooth-flowing (and moderately funky) original. Launched by Brian Faloon's martial snare drill (evoking Ulster's marching bands and military presence), Burns and Cluney strike up an abrupt sequence of percussive guitar sounds, culminating in a scratchy, rapid-fire effect that quickly descends into white noise, power chords and feedback. This unequivocal display of rock muscularity merely serves as a preface, though, to the song's central figure, a staccato, reggae-inflected guitar riff (E–F#–A).

Refracted through the distorting prism of punk rock, the song's plaintive tenor is transformed into belligerent angst, not least by Burns's characteristically terse vocal style, conveying rage (where Marley was mournful) at the demise of the song's eponymous figure, an apparently innocent bystander struck down by 'a stray bullet', and reimagined here as a local boy ('A single shot rings out in the Belfast night!').

Harmonic respite is at least offered in the chorus section (A–Bm–C#m–Bm) that eventually serves as backdrop for the track's lengthy improvised jam, giving the band an opportunity to display the sort of virtuoso musicianship against which – rather ironically – punk had come to define itself. At 3.24, for example, Burns launches into a relatively protracted guitar break (replete with 'showy' hammer-ons) that would certainly have contravened punk's three-chord rulebook.

1979

The various links between punk and reggae are, of course, well documented. Indeed, SLF's decision to cover Marley was very much in homage to Burns's heroes The Clash, who had famously included a version of Junior Murvin's 'Police and Thieves' on their eponymously titled debut album two years earlier. Such gestures – part of punk's wider preoccupation with rasta – had been quickly reciprocated by Marley on the delightfully titled 'Punky Reggae Party' (1977). In this context, SLF's rendition of 'Johnny Was' served as a peculiarly (Northern) Irish intervention in punk's Anglo-Jamaican interface, bestowing a universal resonance to an otherwise parochial album, and underlining the band's commitment to Rock Against Racism, with whom they toured in 1979.

Best Bit: When Burns invites the band to 'Take it down!' (4.00), before launching into a series of reggae guitar chops and apparently improvised vocals.

Though SLF re-engaged with reggae at various points throughout their career (they split in 1982 before relaunching five years later), the genre has been scarcely utilized in Ireland. One rather obvious reason for this is the country's relative absence (until very recently) of African-Caribbean immigrants. Notable exceptions include the late 1970s multi-ethnic outfit Zebra, and Tuam's (embryonic Saw Doctors), Too Much For The White Man. Occasional forays into the field have also been made by acts like The Blades and Sinéad O'Connor. More significantly, when U2 made a triumphant return to the live arena on their 2001 Elevation tour, the band segued extracts of 'Johnny Was' into their key Troubles song 'Sunday Bloody Sunday'. This may have been a well-meaning effort to illuminate postcolonial solidarities, but it also underlined the influence of SLF on subsequent Irish rock; listen again to the opening bars of, say, 'Alternative Ulster' and think of Edge's early fretwork on formative U2 numbers like 'Electric Co.' (1980). In the space of one album, these Belfast punks had not only introduced rasta to Irish rock, they'd also paved the way for the country's premier rock act of the 1980s. Not a bad way to close the decade.

1980

My Perfect Cousin

THE UNDERTONES [SIRE]

The emergence of the punk subculture in mid-1970s London had spawned a multitude of independent record labels, the best known of which was Rough Trade, whose first major release – Stiff Little Fingers' 'Suspect Device' (1978) — had originally been pressed on the group's own Rigid Digits imprint. This 'cottage industry' model of record production was very much in the ascent in late 1970s Belfast, with the city boasting its very own indie label, Good Vibrations, launched by local entrepreneur Terri Hooley and named after his city record store. The first fruits of Hooley's enterprise came in May 1978 with the release of 'Big Time' by Rudi (arguably the city's first punk band), quickly followed by key singles from similarly pop-inflected Northern punk groups like Protex ('Don't Ring Me Up') and The Outcasts ('Justa Nother Teenage Rebel').

Undoubtedly the most notable of Hooley's signings that year, however, was The Undertones from Derry City, a band which had formed four years earlier around guitar-playing brothers John and Damian O'Neill, vocalist Feargal Sharkey, bassist Michael Bradley and drummer Billy Doherty. Initially a rhythm 'n' blues covers band with a residency at Derry's Casbah nightclub, the avowedly DIY ethos of punk had awakened the group to the possibility of developing their own material.

Rock critic Jon Savage would later refer to The Undertones as 'the missing link between The Stooges and Irish traditional music', but the group's exuberant bursts of melodic three-chord punk-pop owed far more to the template of New York's Ramones and Manchester's Buzzcocks than Detroit proto-punk or Dublin diddly-eye. A truly distinctive component of the group's sound, though, was Sharkey's vocal signature, its tremulous modulations only compounded by an audibly regional accent.

The band's predilection for parka anoraks, V-neck sweaters and turned-up jeans, meanwhile, may have been informed by provincial naivety, but signified a resolute ordinariness (one critic famously likened Sharkey to 'an unemployed plumber in a *Play for Today* production') that contrasted starkly with the peroxide and mohair of metropolitan punk: 'Dressed like that you must be living in a different world,' as Sharkey himself put it in 'Get Over You'.

And while the likes of Lydon and Strummer were furiously documenting the political crises and urban anomie overhanging post-imperial Britain (conditions which anyone raised in Derry's Bogside during the early Troubles had experienced first-hand), The Undertones were far more concerned with the vicissitudes of everyday life, offering

light-hearted meditations on the day-to-day experiences of male adolescence. Thus, while fellow Northerners Stiff Little Fingers traded in the furrow-browed social realism of *Inflammable Material* (1979), The Undertones persevered with 'More Songs About Chocolate and Girls', making pioneering references to Subbuteo ('My Perfect Cousin') and eulogizing schoolboy snacks ('Mars Bars'). Most striking in this regard, though, was the group's paean to youthful thrills that served as title track on their justly celebrated *Teenage Kicks* EP in September 1978.

Such was the response to this debut effort (BBC DJ John Peel famously gave it back-to-back airings on his late-night radio show, and continually hailed it as his 'favourite song of all time') that within a matter of weeks the group had been picked up by US

Best Bit: The reference to Subbuteo so memorably evoked in the record's now famous sleeve-design.

major label Sire, who immediately reissued the original EP. Lavish critical praise – as well as numerous *Top of the Pops* performances – ensued as the group continued to mine a perfect pop vein with singles like 'Get Over You', 'Jimmy Jimmy' and 'Here Comes the Summer' in 1979.

The group's biggest chart success, however, came the following spring when they reached the UK Top Ten for the first and only time with 'My Perfect Cousin', a lead-off single for the group's second long-player, *Hypnotised* (1980), a collection that served to consolidate the infectious punk pop of their eponymously titled debut (1979). In keeping with the group's earlier material, the track is on the short side (winding down after only two and a half minutes), and opens with a neat – if rather familiar – ascending guitar figure (G to A, A to E), before a taut rhythm section drops in to add some bottom to the mix. This, in turn, prompts Sharkey's precisely clipped – though heavily accented – spoken-sung delivery ('Now I've got a cousin called Kevin / He's sure to go to Heaven'), instigating a slice-of-life account of seething intra-familial tensions (apparently informed by a degree of actuality: 'Kevin' was based on one of Bradley's over-achieving relatives).

Rather than simple Irish begrudgery, though, the indignation animated by the song's narrator is based on an archetypal teenage experience: that of being craftily shafted by, and then unfavourably compared with, a high-flying peer. Perhaps the song's definitive moment, in this regard, is Sharkey's venomously spat recollection: 'He always beat me at Subbuteo, 'cos he "flicked to kick" and I didn't know!'

As we might expect from The Undertones, however, tender charm ultimately outweighs harsh realism, hence the insertion of a colourful guitar note in the collectively sung chorus that momentarily throws Kevin's litany of misdeeds into sharp relief. Moreover, the playful wit displayed throughout by the song's narrator ('He thinks that I'm a cabbage, 'cos I hate *University Challenge*') effectively serves to redress – if only symbolically – the familial imbalance recounted in the lyric, an attribute that is underscored by the harmonic resolution offered in the song's final bars, which restore the opening guitar figure, replete with reverberating fuzz.

Simplistic buzzsaw guitar riffs were beginning to sound a tad passé at the turn of the new decade, however. In Ireland itself, for example, the fledgling U2 – following the lead of paradigm-shifting 'New Wave' acts in the UK (Joy Division, PiL) and US (Television, Talking Heads) – were preparing to issue their first international single, the Martin Hannett-produced '11 O'Clock Tick Tock' (1980), after a high-profile live performance at the 'Sense of Ireland' festival in London, which had showcased new Irish music for the UK public.

And though The Undertones had berated synth-wielding 'art-school boys' in the lyrics of 'My Perfect Cousin', the group's later efforts *Positive Touch* (1981) and *The Sin of Pride* (1983), released on their own EMI-licensed Ardeck label, saw them venture into the slicker (and less immediately accessible) terrain of brass-augmented designer pop and white-boy soul. In the process, though, The Undertones had alienated their principal fan base, leading to a sharp decline in record sales and the inevitable press backlash.

Disbanding in 1983, Sharkey went on to experience mainstream pop fame – albeit only briefly – with solo efforts 'A Good Heart' (1985) and 'You Little Thief' (1986), while the O'Neill brothers innovated with hard-edged dance rock in That Petrol Emotion. Neither party was capable, though, of reigniting that special affection which fans of melodic punk pop have continued to hold for The Undertones.

Ghost of a Chance

THE BLADES [ENERGY]

The second year of the new decade was a strange one in Ireland. After the trauma of the Stardust nightclub fire – in which forty-four young revellers died at a Dublin disco – there were the protracted IRA hunger strikes, which pitted Republican prisoners against the Thatcher administration in a bitter struggle over political status. On the Iron Lady's own patch, meanwhile, the hoopla of a royal wedding (Charles and Diana) did little to conceal the increasing fragmentation of British society, with record unemployment figures and multiple urban riots offering a stark reminder of that country's internal strife.

While the latter events found poetic expression in The Specials' 'Ghost Town' (1981) – an eerie and uncannily prescient commentary on contemporary British life – it was left to another English group, The Police, to deal with the Ulster crisis on 'Invisible Sun' (1981). Irish rock bands, it seemed, were steering well clear of the Troubles. Admittedly, Derry's Undertones – who famously avoided commenting on the North – mustered a heavily concealed allusion to current events, cunningly wrapped in the delightful pop charm of 'It's Going to Happen!' (1981). But it would take a couple of years before a major Irish rock act like U2 – who made their *Top of the Pops* debut in 1981 – could unleash an overt Troubles tune such as 'Sunday Bloody Sunday' (1983).

This is not to say that Irish rock musicians were eschewing all forms of political commentary. On the contrary, some of the country's finest songwriters were tackling issues far beyond the national question. Thus, on their seminal 'Ghost of a Chance' single (1981), The Blades took on the issue of class, a much-neglected area of Irish political debate. Unlike most of their Dublin contemporaries (The Rats, The Radiators, U2), The Blades had unambiguously working-class origins, hailing from the south Dublin suburb of Ringsend. Formed during the halcyon days of punk in 1977, the band was based around songwriter Paul Cleary (vocals / bass), his older brother Lar (guitar) and drummer Pat Larkin. After a lengthy 1978 residency at Dublin's Magnet Bar (which created a major 'buzz' around their home town), the group secured another high-profile residency slot – with rivals U2 – at the Baggot Inn.

In stark contrast to the latter's early art-rock pretensions, the clean-cut Blades wore sharp suits and cropped hair, evoking a late 1960s Mod aesthetic. Meanwhile, their highly melodic brand of post-punk power pop had more in common with English New Wavers like Squeeze. Presenting themselves as ordinary working-class lads, the band were notoriously uncomfortable doing promotional activities. Cleary in particular displayed a healthy contempt for the machinations of the music business, with its increasing emphasis on fashion, style and hype.

By the turn of the 1980s, the band had gained a nationwide reputation as an exhilarating live act and, after striking a deal with a small English label, Energy, they were quickly tipped for chart success. A debut single, 'Hot for You' (1980), showcased the band's punchy guitar-based pop, but it was the follow-up effort, 'Ghost of a Chance' (1981), that really established The Blades – and especially Cleary – as a major songwriting force. Recorded in London, the lyric finds Cleary back in Dublin, gripped by boredom as his girlfriend takes 'a working trip'. Nothing unusual in that, you might think, just the usual boy-meets-girl, boy-misses-girl type of sentiment that has been standard pop-song fodder since the days of Tin Pan Alley. However, this is early 1980s Dublin – a period of heavy unemployment – and the object of this (working-class) boy's desire is the well-heeled tennis-playing gal graphically imagined on the record sleeve's artwork.

Setting up this tale of love across the great divide, Larkin's echoey snare and Lar's reverberated root-note riff immediately conjure a spacey world of possibility. A high-register vocal ('Long weekend …') furnishes the track with a degree of harmonic contrast, but the tune's upbeat tenor is assuredly maintained by an evenly strummed

....

Best Bit: The carefully layered harmonies in the tight chorus section, thrown into relief only by Lar's jangly guitar motif (D–Dsus4).

....

rhythm guitar part (A–F#m–D–E). As the track unfolds, though, Cleary's lyrics become increasingly incongruous, not least during the memorable chorus section, in which the singer's restrained harmonies ('Not a ghost of a chance / We never had') are counterposed by an uplifting guitar figure, with Lar's simple arpeggio embellishing a steady sequence of dampened major chords (A–E–G–D).

If the singer's pessimism here had been briefly foreshadowed by a tense bridge section ('She sends me postcards / Every now and then'), Cleary is candidly overt about the source of his anxiety, pointing to apparently insurmountable class differences via 'education' and accent ('but to hear her talking …'). Relief is momentarily offered in a neatly executed – and characteristically modest – instrumental break that serves as the track's middle eight (2.17–2.29). However, this jangly A7 sequence proves frustratingly circular, and Cleary's subsequent reiteration of the song's hook line only takes the listener to a fading coda. This subtle blend of frustrated yearning and uplifting harmonies displays a far more refined approach to songwriting than the average post-punk fare, its raw energy tempered by Cleary's measured pop sensibilities and knack for melodic structure.

Though hailed as a classic in Ireland, 'Ghost' failed to register in Britain, where the fragile post-punk consensus had split into pop flamboyancy ('new romantics', Adam And The Ants, *The Face*) and rock existentialism (grey raincoats, Echo And The Bunnymen, *NME*). Cleary's straight-up sincerity and 'old school' songwriting ethic endeared him little to either camp, but a more fundamental problem lay in the fact that The Blades' label, Energy, had folded shortly after the release of 'Ghost'.

Larkin and Lar promptly left the group, with Cleary switching to lead guitar and recruiting replacements Brian Foley (bass) and Jake Reilly (drums). After striking a deal with Irish label Reekus, the band released another piece of classic pop vinyl, 'The Bride Wore White' (1982). Though voted 'Best Single' in that year's *Hot Press* poll (beating off stiff competition from the likes of U2 and Clannad), such success did not translate abroad. Nevertheless, things continued to look up for the band when former Stones manager Andrew Loog Oldham spotted their set at the 1983 Lisdoonvarna music festival and immediately signed the group to US label Elektra.

With veteran producer John Porter (Roxy Music, The Smiths) at the helm, sessions for the band's debut album took an especially soulful turn, introducing a Dexys Midnight Runners-style brass aesthetic (courtesy of horn section Frank Duff and Paul Grimes). Unfortunately, though, the band's US label was abruptly transformed by a series of high-level personnel changes, and the group found themselves once again without a deal. As a consequence, *The Last Man in Europe,* the band's only studio album, received a belated Irish-only release on Reekus in 1985.

Stand-out track 'Downmarket' was hailed as a contemporary Irish classic, its critique of early 1980s Dublin ('Everything's black and white and grey') underlined by Cleary's refusal to play at 1986's Self-Aid benefit show for Ireland's unemployed (the singer felt the event let the Government off the hook). Later that year, the group played a farewell show at Dublin's Olympic Ballroom, concluding their recording career with an anthology, *Raytown Revisited* (1986). Cleary eventually left the music scene altogether, turning his hand to journalism (*Hot Press, In Dublin*) and TV theme tunes, and even devising questions for RTÉ quiz shows. By the turn of the millennium, however, he had returned to the rock fold, with the release of a Blades compilation album, *Those Were the Days* (2000), and a critically acclaimed solo effort, *Crooked Town* (2001). Shortly thereafter, the Republic of Ireland soccer team announced that their traditional pre-match diddly-eye music had been replaced by the sounds of The Blades. Cleary's history of heroic failure couldn't have found a more appropriate home.

Theme from *Harry's Game*

CLANNAD [TARA]

As Ireland was recovering from its coldest winter since the 1930s, the world was facing a period of intense political conflict. In the South Atlantic, British forces were squaring up to General Galtieri after his Argentine army had entered the disputed Falklands/Malvinas territory. Meanwhile, in London, the Provos were engaged in an especially vicious bombing campaign, executing brutal attacks on Hyde Park and Regent's Park.

With violent international hostilities dominating the year's news agenda, the studio-bound U2 elected to call their next record *War* (1983). Characteristically *au fait* with political developments, Bono and the boys were wilfully out of synch with musical trends, which in 1982 meant the high artifice of British synth pop (Duran Duran, The Human League, A Flock Of Seagulls). The band had some interest, however, in the emerging roots-rock movement, which sought out raw authenticity (over glamour and style), as exhibited at 1982's inaugural WOMAD (World Of Music, Arts and Dance) Festival. Significantly, this rootsy turn would spawn a number of Irish-influenced sounds and styles, not least on the year's best-selling single, 'Come on Eileen' by Dexys Midnight Runners, which displayed a distinctly 'Celtic' aesthetic.

It was this tension between traditionalist roots rock and technology-driven synth pop that provided the context for Ireland's most dramatic single of 1982, Clannad's 'Theme from *Harry's Game*'. The band had been an important part of the Irish folk scene since the early 1970s, but despite five studio albums and countless European tours they'd made little impression on mainstream rock. This would all change with '*Harry's Game*' – their first-ever chart single – which went straight into the UK Top Ten at a dizzying No. 5. Like much of Clannad's earlier material, the track was written in their native tongue, and a highly incongruous *Top of the Pops* performance saw lead vocalist Máire Ní Bhraonáin (Moya Brennan) deliver that show's first-ever Irish-language song. This was no small achievement in 1982, an especially fraught year in Anglo-Irish relations, as

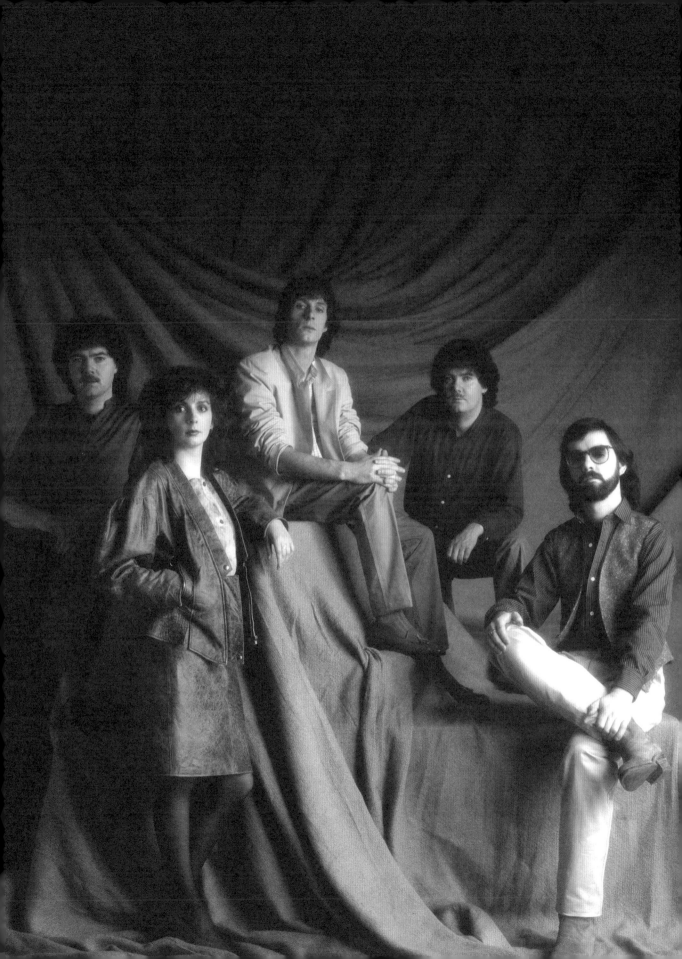

illustrated by the *London Evening Standard*'s now famous publication of a mock film poster advertising 'The Irish: The Ultimate in Psychopathic Horror'.

Singing in Irish had always come naturally to the band, who were raised in an Irish-speaking district of Donegal. And while this may have alienated Anglophone rock fans, classic albums like *Clannad 2* (1974) – issued on the influential Gael Linn label – garnered enormous respect among European folkies (most notably in Germany). They had started off playing cover versions of Beatles songs (translated into Irish) at Leo's Tavern, the family pub in Gweedore. Choosing the name 'Clannad' as an evocation of their shared family background, the band members were all related, with the Bhraonáin siblings Máire (harp, vocals), Pól (flute, guitar, vocals) and Ciarán (bass, guitar, piano, vocals) being joined by twin uncles Pádraig (guitar, mandola, vocals) and Noel Ó Dugáin (guitar, vocals).

Raised by a showband father and choirleader mother (both with experience of ceilidh and big-band set-ups), the Bhraonáins developed a highly eclectic musical palette, listening to rock and jazz as much as folk and trad. But their desire to marry popular and traditional styles was also a symptom of Donegal's peculiar geo-politics. Situated at the northernmost point of the island (yet still in the Republic), the county's inhabitants had access to both British-broadcast rock 'n' roll as well as RTÉ-transmitted diddly-eye. Consequently, the band had little problem incorporating jazz, rock and classical idioms in the framework of their Irish folk aesthetic. But few could have anticipated their remarkable fusion of 1982's divergent musical trends, with '*Harry's Game*' mixing postmodern technology with pre-modern style on a highly affecting Celt-pop hybrid.

Making use of the now legendary Prophet synthesizer, the track fades in quietly with a low-register root note. Barely has this sound been registered when it is overlaid with Máire's ethereal vocal, her striking melody – and distinctly Irish words – evoking the *sean-nós* style of traditional Irish singing. Closely miked and heavily reverberated, the singer's breathy delivery – juxtaposed with a slow-paced, descending synth – creates an especially haunting effect.

Set against this extraordinary backcloth, the song's words function less as semantic carriers of meaning than as sonic evocations of mood. Indeed, a literal English translation suggests that they lack the gravitas implied by the singer's serene delivery. Thus, the first verse roughly translates as 'I will go east and go west / To the places from whence came / The moon and the sun', while the second reads 'The moon and the sun will go / And the young man / With his reputation behind him'. Interestingly, many listeners also assumed that the song's chorus was in Irish, when in fact it merely offered a slow-motion rendition of a classic lilting phrase ('Fol lol the doh fol the day / Fol the doh fol the day').

The success of this wordplay rests upon on a deceptively simple musical structure. During the chorus, for example, the band make use of a highly conventional chord pattern (C#m–B–A–E–A–B) found in classic rock tunes like Elvis Presley's 'Burning Love' (1972). Slowed down to a snail's pace, and masked by multi-layered synth textures and otherworldly choral harmonies, this rudimentary rock figure inadvertently provided the foundation for one of Irish music's most significant points of departure, with 'Harry's Game' signalling the birth of a hybrid new genre that came to be known as 'Celtic New Age'. In this regard, the record anticipated the Enya phenomenon, based around the younger Ní Bhraonáin sister Eithne, who briefly contributed vocals and keyboards to Clannad during the early 1980s (departing just prior to the recording of 'Harry's Game').

Notwithstanding the possible influence of Clannad on Enya – or vice versa – the record dramatically increased the group's profile, picking up an Ivor Novello Award and earning them a major label deal with RCA. Fittingly, as the record had begun life as a soundtrack tune (Harry's Game was a popular TV mini-series about an undercover

Best Bit: The beginning of the third verse (1.50– 2.03), with Máire's dramatic vocal ('Imtheochaidh a dtainig ariamh') heightened by multiple layers of descending synth-bass.

spy in Northern Ireland), the band quickly found their niche as producers of film and television music. Thus, Legend (1984) was commissioned for a British TV show about Robin Hood, while 'Harry's Game' itself became – ten years after its original release – the soundtrack for a major Hollywood movie, Patriot Games (1992). Since then, it has been used in numerous television commercials around the globe. And though Clannad would achieve only one other major chart success – a stirring collaboration with Bono on 'In a Lifetime' (1986) – they will forever be remembered as the pioneers of that trademark 'Celtic' soundscape.

Steel Claw

PAUL BRADY [POLYDOR]

Like his fellow Northern Irishman Van Morrison, Paul Brady is an interesting figure in the context of this book insofar as he more or less spans the entire time period covered. Indeed, even more than his highly acclaimed and better-known compatriot, you could tell the story of Irish rock music just by tracing Brady's career trajectory over the past forty years.

Brady grew up listening to a wide variety of popular music styles at home in Strabane and at school in Derry. Having taught himself guitar and piano, he spent some time playing at tourist-town hotels before moving to Dublin to attend university in 1965. Once there, he quickly tapped into the burgeoning scene, and began to make a mark with local beat heroes Rootsgroup and The Kult before starting his own band, Rockhouse. His encounter and subsequent fascination during the late 1960s with folk and traditional music is well documented. Periods with The Johnstons, Planxty, Andy Irvine and as a solo performer followed, culminating in 1978's award-winning *Welcome Here Kind Stranger* album. More than a decade's immersion in trad (disregarding a couple of 'lost' years in the US) left him widely regarded as one of the most talented and important performers within the field. Musically, however, Brady felt increasingly unfulfilled, and it was at that point that he rediscovered his rock 'n' roll roots, and began to write, perform and eventually record his own original music in the pop/rock idiom.

If the folk and trad fraternity were horrified (not quite 'Judas' terrain but certainly heading in that direction), the end seemed to justify the decision in as much as Brady's first rock album, *Hard Station* (1981), remains one of the definitive statements of modern Irish popular music. This self-penned debut is perhaps one of the first sustained collections of songs which speaks directly to the modern Irish condition in the language of rock 'n' roll (a point, by the way, routinely missed by those who regard Brady as a sort of poor man's Van). At the same time, a ten-year affair with traditional music had obviously left a strong imprint upon him, and it's there to be heard in many different aspects of the music: the lyrical phrasing, the strong melodies, the head-on projection and the controlled vocal style, the hint of an Ulster accent at the corner of various words, and the way the writer constructs narratives that draw the listener into particular worlds and situations. The influence is there also in Brady's determination to engage with the real issues and dilemmas that confront real people – much of the time, real Irish people. While a track such as 'The Promised Land' speaks the universal language of love frustrated by circumstance and doubt, there's little in the canon to equal the sheer venom of a specifically Irish-oriented song like 'Nothing But the Same Old Story'.

All in all, Brady revealed himself on *Hard Station* to be an intensely reflective man who felt things deeply and was in desperate need of a medium through which to express his responses to life as he encountered it. After that first album his talent was not in doubt, but people also sensed the integrity and the commitment underpinning his music.

Somewhat disappointed by the limited response to *Hard Station,* and not a little disgusted by the realities of the rock business, Brady moved to England in the winter of 1982 to record his second rock album with Neil Dorfsman, a producer who had recently worked with A-list acts such as Dire Straits and Bruce Springsteen. Whereas *Hard Station* was a more or less spontaneous statement on Brady's new direction and included material gathered during his trad period, the second album raised difficult questions (as it so often does) about range, intent and audience. The record's eight tracks found him settling into the groove he has occupied more or less ever since – soulfully performed,

Best Bit: 'It doesn't really matter when you're crawling in the gutter ...' – the timeless logic of the oppressed.

well-crafted music for the mature listener. 'Helpless Heart', a beautiful ballad about temporary separation, has proved particularly popular, and has been covered by such luminaries as Phil Collins and David Crosby (not to mention Johnny Logan). This kind of music is not everyone's cup of tea, of course, but the niche is there and it's as well to have someone as talented and thoughtful as Brady occupying it.

'Steel Claw' is a song of its time and place, which is to say, Dublin in the early 1980s. The post-Tiger generations may not be aware of the fact, but the 1980s was one of the bleakest periods in modern Irish history. 'Hard times all around', as the title track from *Hard Station* had it – a time of unemployment, emigration, recession and, most seriously of all, a widespread lack of hope for the future. Pre-Temple Bar Dublin was the dead centre of the malaise. Unscrupulous gangsters flooded the joy-riding projects with cheap heroin, creating an epidemic of addiction and an ensuing crime wave as the drug became more difficult to find and more expensive to buy. It was the 'steel claw' of poverty and privilege. It was a situation U2 would describe as 'bad' on the following year's *Unforgettable Fire.* It was a tribunal waiting to happen. It was a situation that was eventually relieved more by shifting global economic patterns than by any concerted effort on the part of local or central governments.

1983

In terms of mood and sound, 'Steel Claw' revisits the ground broached in 'Busted Loose' and 'Nothing But the Same Old Story' from *Hard Station*. While unmistakably of the 1980s, it manages to avoid the characteristic bombast of the period by dint of the singer's obvious sincerity and passion (check out Tina Turner's version from *Private Dancer* (1984) to hear how it might have all gone wrong). The anger expressed in the lyric is supported by the frenetic vocal, the fast tempo and the super-charged, guitar-driven accompaniment. Like the ballads Brady had performed with such conviction and skill in an earlier guise, 'Steel Claw' is a song *of* the people and *for* the people – a folk song, in fact, but one impelled by all the energy and excitement of rock 'n' roll. Deeply familiar as he was with the two traditions, possibly only he could have conceived, written and performed such a song.

Brady will never be up there in the front ranks along with Van, Rory, Philo and Bono, but if there is such a thing as a distinctive Irish rock style – in which music, lyrics and most importantly *mood* appear to answer something deep within the national psyche – then songs such as 'Steel Claw' embody it as well as any other you may care to suggest.

Loftholdingswood

MICRODISNEY [STRANGE FRUIT]

Although 1984 failed to bring about the dystopian nightmare predicted by George Orwell, there was still plenty to be concerned about, with the New Right's tightening grip on global politics (via the Reagan-Thatcher nexus), continuing Apartheid in South Africa and famine in Ethiopia. Irish society, for its part, offered a number of high-profile responses to this sorry state of affairs, with street protests against Reagan on his visit to Ireland, a boycott of South African goods at Dunnes Stores and Bob Geldof's legendary Band Aid project for famine relief.

The latter's pop career had fallen into serious decline, with Rats numbers like 'Tonight' (1984) and 'Drag Me Down' (1984) failing to reach the UK Top Forty. From a specifically Irish perspective, the Rats had been well and truly eclipsed by U2, who were now able to offer a helping hand to Ireland's up-and-coming young rock bands. Mindful of the difficulties they'd had securing a record deal, Bono and the boys set up the Mother Records imprint, offering short-term start-up deals to aspirant local acts. It was difficult to fault the project's altruism, though its early beneficiaries – In Tua Nua, Cactus World News – were hardly at the cutting-edge of Ireland's mid-1980s rock scene.

Had Bono and Co. looked further afield, they might have discovered a far more novel strand of popular-music-making. The city of Cork will forever be associated with virtuoso bluesman Rory Gallagher, but since the late 1970s it had also been home to a rather eccentric art-rock experiment that would eventually give Cork a reputation for oddball indie pop. Instigated in the late 1970s by groups like Nun Attax and Five Go Down To The Sea?, this quirky Cork tradition first came to public attention in the mid-1980s with Stump, whose anarchic shambling paved the way for 1990s bands like The Frank and Walters and Sultans of Ping FC. At the very heart of this left-field Cork project was another – altogether more serious – outfit called Microdisney.

Formed in 1980 by Cathal Coughlan (vocals, keyboards) and Sean O'Hagan (guitar), the duo's early 'cabaret punk' phase eventually gave way to an expanded five-piece project trading in fast-paced garage funk. By 1982, with the band's rhythm section seceding to form Stump, Coughlan and O'Hagan were able to launch Microdisney proper. Taking an increasingly stylized approach to songwriting and production, the duo drew on an eclectic range of sources including Brian Wilson, America, Van Dyke Parks and Steely Dan. Such refined pop sensibilities were always counterposed with Coughlan's abrasive polemicism, his lyrics offering a subversive – and often surreal – take on contemporary affairs. Cultivating a notoriously combative persona, Coughlan's bilious invective (he famously described U2 as 'scum') came to life during the group's belligerent, drink-fuelled live shows.

Microdisney's trademark juxtaposition of bright melody with harsh message made for an interesting sound – 'a manifesto of anger set to a happy beat', as *Record Mirror* put it. However, this stylistic paradox left the group in a rather anomalous position between rock's margins and mainstream. Too accessible to be 'alternative', yet too acerbic for mass acceptance, they were denied both unconditional critical praise and proper chart recognition.

Microdisney began their career with buckets of street cred, however, after BBC DJ John Peel picked up on early single 'Pink Skinned Man' (1983). Issued on Kabuki Records – set up in London to support young Irish rock bands – they struck a deal with über-indie label Rough Trade for their facetiously titled debut album *Everybody Is Fantastic* (1984). With the band now based in London, the album soon found its way into the UK's fledgling indie chart. However, Rough Trade's limited resources were increasingly taken up by the emergent Smiths, and with little support for new studio material, the band issued a stopgap compilation of older songs. Released under the contentious

Best Bit: The final bridge section (3.37–3.52) in which the boy/'girl' duet fully realizes the song's surreal country-rock aesthetic.

title *We Hate You South African Bastards!* (1984), these early singles and unreleased demos took Microdisney to the UK indie Top Ten. However, the now penniless duo were still awaiting record-company support, and faced with an increasingly uncertain future, they turned to rock's most famous hallucinogen, LSD. (In fairness, they had always professed an interest in 'the psychedelic side of country music'). In any case, this period of experimentation had a transformative effect on the band, giving them a heightened perspective on mid-1980s London, with its burgeoning materialism and increasingly right-wing politics.

Out of this difficult period came the excellent *In the World* EP (1985), the band's first new material since recruiting a full-time rhythm section and keyboard player. Its slow-paced lead-off number 'Loftholdingswood' had been showcased a year earlier during one of the group's John Peel radio sessions. This definitive version of the track begins with a warmth synth motif, its subtle modulation between Gm and Gm6 underpinned by O'Hagan's quietly dampened electric. This sets the scene for a rather languid verse in which Coughlan's low-register vocal trails a gently strummed acoustic guitar (B♭–C–E♭m–F–D–E♭) and punctuating bass drum. The singer's barely comprehensible lyrics offer a string of apparently random images ('the sesame store', 'bluebells shine'), including 'Loftholdingswood', the song's enigmatic title.

Picking up for a country-style bridge section (Am–C–G–Am–C–D), O'Hagan's bright, heavily chorused guitar illuminates the track's murky mix, while his Scotty Moore-style licks enliven the band's weary pace. Such buoyancy is inevitably offset by Coughlan's acerbic words, with the singer offering an iconoclastic aside to his country's religiosity ('I died on a cross / and now I'm the boss'). The band had always kicked against Catholic Ireland's religious superstition – most notably on 'Helicopter of the Holy Ghost' (1983) – and this was only exacerbated by the mid-1980s vogue for 'moving' statues in Cork and Kerry. However, 'Loftholdingswood' is ultimately more concerned with phoney English liberalism than Irish 'sacred cows', hence the singer's derisive chiding – in the relatively upbeat chorus – of his privileged addressee: 'Aren't you glad you were born in England? / Aren't you glad you were born an angel? / That's why you think you see / Everywhere struggles to be free.'

An equally enigmatic second verse conjures images of gambling ('Dan McGrath', 'the racing form') and alcoholism ('brandy glass', 'liver gave up'), before Coughlan is joined by the backing vocalist's octave melody (contributing to the song's country and western conceit). After further arcane references ('Edgeware Road', 'Lebanon'), the song restores its original synth/guitar intro, while Coughlan launches into a surreal spoken rant, caustically repeating the nonsense phrase 'rupture demenstract', pronouncing the latter word to rhyme with 'democrat'. This peculiar dialogue eventually signals the song's fading coda, in which the singer draws out the sonoric features of the song's title ('Lofting, Loftholdingswood …'). Offering little in the way of denouement, the song – as part of the *In the World* EP – returned Microdisney to the indie Top Ten, paving the way for their next long-player, *The Clock Comes Down the Stairs* (1985). An indie No. 1, this album led to a deal with Virgin for follow-up effort *Crooked Mile* (1987). Both records showcased some fine material, but suffered from ill-fitting production. While *Clock* was held back by a rather murky mix (in which Coughlan's previously discernible accent was largely buried), *Crooked Mile* was too slickly orchestrated, with producer Lenny Kaye's lush textures making for an excessively polished sound.

'Town to Town' (1987), the latter's lead-off single, was a classic 1980s pop tune (attracting mainstream TV exposure and a prestigious U2 support slot), but bizarrely failed to reach the UK Top Forty. In the meantime, the band became increasingly unhappy with the album's production, and refused to issue any further singles from the set. Taking full responsibility for (what they saw as) the record's shortcomings, they immediately set to work on new material. However, after just one more long-player, *39 Minutes* (1988), they finally decided to call it a day, issuing T-shirts with the slogan 'Microdisney are shit' to announce the split. Though Coughlan and O'Hagan continued to mine a left-field indie vein with Fatima Mansions and The High Llamas respectively, they are best remembered as Microdisney – Ireland's most enigmatic, uncompromising and downright demanding rock duo.

Take My Hand

IN TUA NUA [ISLAND]

By the mid-1980s, the Irish Republic had become a country with a 'third-world' economy, with a quarter of a million unemployed and as many as 30,000 people emigrating in a single year. While Dublin struggled to cope with industrial unrest and an emerging heroin epidemic, the centre of Belfast was filled with angry Unionists supporting Ian Paisley's 'Ulster Says No' campaign, an unequivocal riposte to 1985's historic Anglo-Irish Agreement. These trying times were at least tempered by the island's prosperous cultural life, with the Irish rugby team securing a famous Triple Crown victory and Barry McGuigan winning the World Featherweight boxing title. In rock music, too, things seemed to be looking up, as witnessed by U2's triumphant homecoming show at Dublin's Croke Park in June 1985 (not to mention their memorable Live Aid set two weeks later). In truth, however, Ireland's rock scene was far from vibrant, with the great bands of the late 1970s – Lizzy, The Rats, SLF, The Undertones – all effectively disbanded, and the ascendant U2 casting a long shadow over any potential newcomers. Indeed, the only Irish act to feature on the latter's Croke Park support bill was In Tua Nua, hardly an ideal example of innovative 1980s rock.

They'd been 'discovered' by Bono in 1983, when the singer had been out for a quiet pint in Howth ahead of U2's performance at the 'Day at the Races' festival in Phoenix Park. Fronted by lead singer Leslie Dowdall – Irish rock's first female sex symbol – the band had been launched in 1982 by Martin Clancy (guitar, keyboards) and Ivan O'Shea (guitar). After a trial period with a precocious teenage singer called Sinéad O'Connor, they'd settled on the more experienced – and rock-oriented – vocals of Dowdall. With Paul Byrne (drums) and Jack Dublin (bass) furnishing the group's classic rock backcloth, it was left to Steve Wickham (fiddle) and Vinnie Kilduff (uilleann pipes, tin whistle) to supply some sparkle to the mix.

The latter pair were already on their way to becoming local session 'stars', with Wickham contributing fiddle parts to U2's *War* (1983), and Kilduff playing pipes and bodhrán on *October* (1981). But In Tua Nua were far from being an 'old school' trad outfit. Indeed, of Ireland's notable 1980s fusion acts – Moving Hearts, Stockton's Wing – they were the most straightforwardly rock-based, displaying an especially obvious debt to West Coast acts like Jefferson Airplane (whom they covered on 1985's 'Somebody to Love').

Like many Celtic rock bands, theirs was a sound that worked best in the outdoors, hence their many festival dates with the likes of U2 and Simple Minds, not to mention an early (and highly prestigious) support slot at Bob Dylan's Slane show in 1984. Kick-starting a bill that included Santana and UB40, the Nua had only just released their debut single, 'Coming Thru'' (1984). Recorded at Eamonn Andrews's Studio in Dublin, the record was the first fruit of U2's Mother Records project. Launched in 1984 as a start-up label for new Irish bands, Mother enabled local acts to make inroads into the global music scene with that most tangible of rock documents: a piece of recorded vinyl. Its first experiment – 'Coming Thru'' – was largely successful, with In Tua Nua being quickly picked up by Island Records after their legendary Slane show.

Whilst demoing material for their new label, one track in particular stood out. 'Take My Hand' had originally been issued as the B-side of 'Coming Thru'', having been co-written with Sinéad O'Connor during the band's formative period. With a reworked arrangement, and a slower than original tempo, 'Take My Hand' became the group's international debut single in 1985. Fading in with a reverse-effect crash cymbal, the track displays an epic sweep that has 'film soundtrack' written all over it. Based on a deceptively simple blues figure (Em–Dm–Am), Clancy's haunting synth provides an ethereal backdrop for the band's simple melody – performed on fiddle, tin whistle and piano – evoking the Far East as much as the American West (albeit within a distinctively Irish idiom). This relatively lengthy intro (49 seconds) sets the scene for Dowdall's sturdy vocal ('Lonely man / Tired man / Play the blues'), with the band switching to a different chord sequence (Dm–C–Am–G) for the verse. Accompanied only by piano and synth, the singer's highly controlled mid-register delivery sounds a little strained, with Dowdall striving for power and precision, rather than passion or punch. Indeed, certain lines are distinguished only by their echoey reverberation or American-style pronunciation, pointing to a distinctly AOR aesthetic.

The downbeat chorus (Em–G–F–Am–G) is at least enlivened by a few crashing cymbals, with Dowdall's octave-spanning vocals drawing out a fundamentally weak lyric ('Take my hand / Take my hand / Lie on sand / Rest on sand'). Later sections are augmented by a modest but effective fretless bass, which provides a fairly impressive – and heavily chorused – solo during the track's finale. Fading out with a brief tin whistle flourish, the track was an unusual choice for the band's international debut single, with Sinéad O'Connor apparently claiming that the tune benefited little from its new tempo and arrangement.

Notwithstanding Sinéad's feelings about the band, it's interesting that In Tua Nua became better known for the work of their ex-members than for the merits of their own output. This was in large part due to a series of high-level personnel changes, creative false starts and soured relationships. Shortly after the deal with Island, Wickham was poached by Mike Scott's Waterboys and – with Kilduff departing shortly thereafter – the band's projected debut album was cancelled. Finding themselves without a label, all the group had to show for their efforts was an Island compilation, *Somebody to Love* (1986). Nevertheless, they were soon buoyed by replacement members Angela De Burca

Best Bit: Jack Dublin's sedate bass solo (4.34–4.51), providing a welcome antidote to Dowdall's overwrought vocal.

(violin) and Brian O'Brien (pipes, sax), striking a deal with Virgin for debut album proper *Vaudeville* (1987). Incorporating classical, folk and Celtic styles into a middle-of-the-road rock aesthetic, it included the Irish hit single 'Seven into the Sea' (1986). Follow-up effort *The Long Acre* (1988) consolidated its predecessor's success, before Virgin flew the group to America for a third album. Working alongside established pop writers like Billy Steinberg – author of Madonna's 'Like a Virgin' (1984) – the record was prematurely billed as In Tua Nua's big 'breakthrough' album. During their stay in the US, however, relationships became increasingly strained and – after spending six months working on what would've been their third album – the project collapsed amidst bitter recriminations and protracted legal disputes. By the end of 1989 the septet from Howth had finally liquidized. Seven into the sea, indeed.

A Rainy Night in Soho

THE POGUES [STIFF]

Popular music in most contemporary societies has been shaped by people who find themselves on the social margins, most notably immigrants and their immediate descendants. This has certainly been the case in Britain, where musicians of immediate Irish descent – from Lonnie Donegan to Noel Gallagher – have played a definitive role. (Think of Lennon and McCartney, Dusty Springfield, John Lydon, Kate Bush, Elvis Costello, Kevin Rowland, Boy George, Morrissey and Marr.)

Few of these artists were as overtly Irish, however, as Shane MacGowan's Pogues, who wore their ethnicity on their collective sleeve at a time when it was neither profitable nor popular. Emerging from the North London pub circuit in the early 1980s – initially under the aegis of Pogue Mahone – the band cooked up a radical fusion of English punk and Irish folk, becoming an unlikely meeting point between The Clancy Brothers and The Clash. MacGowan – who was born in England of Irish parents – had previously gained a degree of notoriety as a prominent 'face' on the London punk scene, not least as lead singer with The Nips, who produced one of the era's classic singles, 'Gabrielle' (1979). By the early 1980s, however, The Nips had disbanded, and with punk's subversive energy in decline Shane turned to the emergent 'world music' scene, which offered a refreshing alternative to the sterile forms of synth pop that now dominated the UK charts.

Observing this trend for Latino and African sounds, MacGowan returned to the 'roots' music of his childhood (much of which was spent in rural Tipperary), explaining that 'if people are being "ethnic", I might as well be my own "ethnic"'. With this in mind, MacGowan recruited a couple of other second-generation Irish musicians, Cait O'Riordan (bass) and Andrew Ranken (drums), as well as a number of non-Irish friends: former Nip James Fearnley (accordion), Jem Finer (banjo) and Spider Stacy (tin whistle).

The group made their live debut in October 1982, and within a couple of years had released a critically acclaimed long-player, *Red Roses for Me* (1984). Though texturally quite spartan and narrow in range, the album showcased MacGowan's extraordinary vocal style – equal parts Luke Kelly and John Lydon – while his lyrical flair evoked the boisterous spirit of Irish writer Brendan Behan.

Perhaps unsurprisingly, the band developed a reputation as a rowdy (and often shambolic) touring outfit, whose live shows were transformed into mass celebrations by alcohol-fuelled fans decked out in Celtic shirts and Irish tricolours. In the process, MacGowan became – in the words of *Hot Press* scribe Eamonn McCann – 'the first [London-Irishman] to give defiant and poetic expression to a community which had never really felt able to proclaim itself'. This was no small achievement in Thatcher's Britain, where anti-Irish prejudice had become a routine response to the Provos' vicious bombing campaign.

The group continued their innovative venture into Celtic folk-punk on *Rum, Sodomy and the Lash* (1985), their Elvis Costello-produced sophomore effort. By this stage, the band had augmented their line-up with the inclusion of ex-Radiators guitarist Phil Chevron, and the album displayed an increasing maturity in terms of style, delivery and musical range, whilst consolidating the group's iconic status amongst the Irish in Britain. Their music was not the sole preserve of Irish migrants, however, for the

Best Bit: The epic sweep of the opening moments, which offer a distinctively Irish melody in a broad, panoramic setting.

band had also been championed by the arbiters of Britain's 'alternative' scene, most notably John Peel (who voted them 'Best Soul Act' of 1984). Not everybody, though, was comfortable with (what many saw as) MacGowan's rehabilitation of the 'drunken Paddy', particularly in Ireland itself, where scenes of the band banging metal beer trays against their heads presumably did little to quell such concerns.

Indeed, something of a controversy was brewing in Dublin folk circles as to the credibility of these London punks hammering away at 'trad' with all the grace of a pissed-up navvy. This debate reached an unseemly climax in 1985 when ex-Planxty man Noel Hill described The Pogues – in an RTÉ radio interview with the band – as 'a terrible abortion' of Irish music, whilst also casting aspersions on the group's 'Irishness'. Notwithstanding such derision, The Pogues had sufficiently impressed their 'home' audience to be invited to play at the following year's Self-Aid concert (a Live-Aid style charity show staged in Dublin for Ireland's unemployed, and featuring acts like U2, Van Morrison and The Boomtown Rats).

A couple of months prior to the Self-Aid date, the band had released their most refined – and commercially successful – effort to date: a four-track EP entitled *Poguetry in Motion* (1986). By this stage, the group's personnel had been bolstered further with the introduction of ex-Sweeney's Men/Steeleye Span/Woods Band instrumentalist Terry Woods. With his supplementary expertise, and Elvis Costello once again at the helm, The Pogues began to experiment with more eclectic terrain. Thus, *Poguetry* begins with the Zydeco-Motown fusion of 'London Girl' and ends with 'Planxty Noel Hill', a frenzied 'trad' riposte to the eponymous purist. The record's obvious stand-out track, though, was 'A Rainy Night in Soho'.

Launched by a striking tin-whistle melody, 'Rainy Night' remix signalled the beginning of a more refined Pogues sound, its multi-layered textures and nuanced arrangement masking a deceptively simple structure (essentially C–F–G ad infinitum). Set at a more considered pace than before, MacGowan's unusually tender vocals – in tandem with the band's unprecedented use of piano, strings and brass – create an especially wistful mood. The lyric, meanwhile, sees MacGowan eulogizing a long-standing romance: 'I've been loving you a long time,' he opines in the opening line, 'Down all the years, down all the days.'

Expressing genuine affection for his addressee ('And I've cried for all your troubles / Smiled at your funny little ways'), MacGowan's sentiment stands in stark contrast to the song's seedy setting (a London red-light district, conjured by the track's intermittent sax motif). The 'ginger lady by [his] bed', meanwhile, appears to be a reference to Victoria Clarke, Shane's long-term partner, who later featured on the sleeve of 'Rainy Night' when it was released as a single in its own right in 1991. However, MacGowan has implied elsewhere that it was whiskey rather than women that he had in mind here.

Ultimately, though, the song appears (without getting too postmodern) to be about itself. Thus, in the penultimate line, MacGowan teasingly informs the listener that 'the song is nearly over / We may never find out what it means'. This playful self-reflexivity only underlines the track's elusive charm, but the final line ('Still there's a light I hold before me / You're the measure of my dreams') packs an emotional punch that is anything but ironic.

The refined eclecticism of *Poguetry* would come to fruition on the band's landmark third album, *If I Should Fall from Grace with God* (1988). The commercial success of its (now canonical) lead-off single, 'Fairytale of New York' (1987), propelled the band into rock's premier league, securing them a prestigious support slot on Bob Dylan's 1988 US tour. Unfortunately, though, Shane's legendary alcohol (and alleged drug) abuse was beginning to take its toll, and the group were forced to tour the US without him. Though MacGowan quickly returned to the fold, subsequent efforts *Peace and Love* (1989) and *Hell's Ditch* (1990) were below par, and Shane's poor health continued to disrupt the band's busy schedule. By 1991, MacGowan had been replaced by former Clash front man Joe Strummer, and a decade would pass before Shane fronted The Pogues on a reunion tour. Nevertheless, throughout the 1990s MacGowan carved out an interesting (if somewhat uneven) solo career, and he continues to be revered – by figures no less than Bono, Sinéad O'Connor and Christy Moore – as one of the greatest Irish songwriters of all time. Noel Hill, for his part, can eat his hat.

1987

Big Decision

THAT PETROL EMOTION [POLYDOR]

Nineteen-eighty-seven was a landmark year in the history of Irish music. In March, veteran folkies The Dubliners celebrated their twenty-fifth anniversary with a *Late Late Show* special, featuring guest appearances by U2, The Pogues and former Taoiseach Charlie Haughey. In early May, housewives' favourite Johnny Logan won the Eurovision Song Contest for a record second time. In between these momentous folk and pop occasions, Irish rock went global with the release of U2's multi-million-selling *Joshua Tree*.

Aside from such high-profile developments, there were a number of significant interventions from Ireland's left field – not least Microdisney, who had a minor UK hit with 'Town to Town' (1987), and The Stars of Heaven, whose *Before Holyhead* EP (1987) marked a creative peak. Even more noteworthy was the pioneering verve of That Petrol Emotion's 'Big Decision' (1987), its hybrid indie/dance fusion predating the UK's 'Madchester' scene – now credited with that invention – by a good two years.

The band had been launched in Derry in 1984 by ex-Undertones guitarist John O'Neill and local DJ/guitar-player Raymond Gorman. O'Neill's brother Damian quickly picked up bass duties, before Ciaran McLaughlin came in on drums. Early interest from Alan McGee's ultra-hip Creation label took the group to London, where they performed a couple of shows as the curiously named Novacaine Combo. US-born singer Steve Mack completed the line-up, before the band fashioned a new name – That Petrol Emotion – a succinct and highly emotive index for the overwhelming sense of frustration and rage felt by the residents of 1980s Derry.

Marking a distinct shift away from The Undertones' unashamed escapism, The Petrols set themselves up as an 'alternative information service', counteracting (what they saw as) the media's mishandling of the Troubles. Band leader O'Neill, the previously reticent chief Undertone, now felt compelled to express the views of disenfranchised nationalists, offering his support for an anti-sectarian All-Ireland Socialist Republic. As a consequence, the band's record sleeves contained polemical tracts on British misconduct in Ireland, recalling the liner notes of early 1980s anarcho-punk outfits like Crass and Conflict. Thus, 'It's a Good Thing' (1986) documented the security forces' use of plastic bullets, while 'Big Decision' (1987) castigated the jury-less Diplock courts. *Manic Pop Thrill* (1986), meanwhile, included extracts from Michael Davitt's *The Fall of Feudalism in Ireland* (1904). Such overt social commentary was underlined by the

group's song lyrics, with tracks like 'Tightlipped' (1986) attacking the media's role in the Troubles, and 'Circusville' (1986) charging Ulster Unionists with sectarianism ('Poison is all that you've spread / Are you proud of the bigots you've bred?'). Meanwhile, the band's newly Gaelicized nomenclature (Seán Ó Néill, Reámann Ó Gormáin, etc.) underscored their openly partisan character.

If this was a reaction against The Undertones' apolitical past, the band also served as a rejoinder to their own musical present, offering a hard-edged riposte to the jangly guitar consensus of mid-1980s indie-pop (as epitomised on *NME*'s now legendary 'C86' collection). Cultivating a refreshingly noisy aesthetic, the band's reference points lay in experimental US garage rock (Captain Beefheart, Pere Ubu), though Ó Néill's spiky guitar lines were always tempered by an infectious pop hook or compelling dance groove. This heady mix made for a frenetic live experience, with the band quickly picking up a one-record deal with Pink, who immediately issued debut single 'Keen' (1985). Although its guitar motif bore more than a passing resemblance to The Smiths' 'Hand in Glove' (1983), the record was critically applauded, with old pal John Peel offering the band some much-needed media exposure on his late-night radio show. Follow-up 'V2' (1986) was issued on the band's own NoiseaNoise label, before they eventually settled on UK indie label Demon. A catchy lead-off single, 'It's a Good Thing' (1986), paved the way for debut long-player *Manic Pop Thrill*, which quickly reached the top of the UK indie chart.

Despite this early success, the band once again switched labels, striking a deal with Polydor for second album *Babble* (1987). Famously described by *Rolling Stone* magazine as 'The Clash crossed with Creedence Clearwater', the set was less convincing than its predecessor. However, stand-out tracks 'Swamp' and 'Big Decision' were among the band's finest, with the latter taking their grungy riff-based rock into largely uncharted dance terrain. This was no mean feat in mid-1980s Britain, where a fairly intense indie/dance stand-off had culminated in Morrissey's memorable 'Hang the DJ!' refrain on The Smiths' 'Panic' (1986). The Petrols, however, had little time for such musical sectarianism, with 'Big Decision' offering an unashamed fusion of hip hop and rock.

Propelled by Seán Ó Néill's cheeky guitar boogie – a mid-register three-note riff (B–G#–D) embellished by some bluesy string bending – the song finds a steady groove in Ó Gormáin's chunky strumming and McLaughlin's simple snare (its rigid echo sounding suspiciously like the drum machine that supplies the track's hand-clap effects). Mack's alluring vocal, meanwhile, is delicately restrained, his soft melodic lines ensuring that the song's polemicism doesn't overwhelm. Consequently, a line about 'plastic bullets' passes almost unnoticed, while the vivid image of 'scum [booting] down the door' garners not so much shock as heartfelt concern.

Belying its ostensibly romantic setting ('See my honey in the streets'), 'Big Decision' served as a clarion call to Northern Irish youth, encouraging potential emigrants to stay put and help resolve the increasingly bitter political crisis (1987 was, after all, the year of the appalling Enniskillen bomb). Thus, while certain lines ('Economies get weaker / Reactionaries stronger') resonated with global events (not least the US stockmarket crash and Thatcher's UK election victory), they were actually a lament for the effects of Ireland's 'brain drain'.

In countering this desire to leave, the song remains appropriately fixed on its 'home chord' (B), with Mack's vocal melody providing subtle harmonic shifts in the verse section. The song does, however, make a chordal detour in the chorus (A–E–B–D–E–B), as Mack's memorable hook drives the song's point home: 'You rather sail the ocean / Than make a big decision.'

Later on, a high-register guitar break (F#–A–G#–B) prefaces the singer's breathless rap ('You gotta agitate / Educate / Organize'). Borrowed from Brother D and the Collective Effort's 'How We Gonna Make the Black Nation Rise?' (1980), the song's desire for political action is made explicit. As well as reworking rap's past, this section also prefaces rock's future, with its single reverberating barre chord anticipating Primal Scream's identical motif on 'Loaded' (1990), a song widely regarded as indie pop's first dance venture. This blending of rock and dance aesthetics arguably made

Best Bit: Mack's startling rap segment (1.17–1.26), giving hip hop an Irish flavour a good five years before The House Of Pain.

for The Petrols' finest moment. However, 'Big Decision' stalled at No. 43 in the UK charts, narrowly missing a crucial Top Forty profile. The band's forthright politics had undoubtedly played a part in curbing their chart potential, with Petrols' liner notes frequently generating tabloid hysteria and even a BBC ban.

This uncompromising attitude also helped little in record company boardrooms, with the band changing labels yet again for their third album, *The End of the Millennium Blues* (1988), a commercial failure that – with the exception of the wonderful 'Cellophane' – failed to impress critics. When Ó Néill left the band prior to the record's tour, The Petrols' days were obviously numbered and – despite taking an increasingly grungy turn (Mack was, after all, from Seattle) – subsequent efforts *Chemicrazy* (1990) and *Fireproof* (1993) failed to sell. Shortly thereafter, the band wisely folded, leaving Irish rock with some of its most radical and inventive material. It's more than you can say for Feargal Sharkey …

Don't Go

HOTHOUSE FLOWERS [LONDON]

The unprecedented success of U2's *Joshua Tree* (1987) increased the level of international attention paid to Irish rock music, giving a tremendous boost to the self-confidence of the domestic music scene, which now had a model of global success (far exceeding that of Van, Lizzy or the Rats) on its own doorstep. Perhaps as a consequence of this increasing sense of self-confidence – bolstered further by the Republic of Ireland's victory over England in the 1988 European Championships – many of the bands that basked in U2's reflected glory were beginning to display a distinctively Irish sound.

Indeed, while Bono and The Edge spent much of 1988 tracing their own musical 'roots' in American blues, country and gospel music (as documented on the poorly received *Rattle and Hum* album and movie), a number of other high-profile Irish-based musicians were mining a source located much closer to home. This was, after all, the year that witnessed Van's extraordinary collaboration with ambassadors of 'trad' The Chieftains on *Irish Heartbeat,* as well as The Waterboys' transformation from 'big music' Scot-rockers to raggle-taggle Celtic folkies on *Fisherman's Blues,* not to mention the creative zenith of The Pogues' punky-Irish fusion on *If I Should Fall from Grace with God.*

Undoubtedly the most notable young Irish group to emerge from this 'Celtic' moment, though, was Dublin's Hothouse Flowers, who had been hailed (by no less a source than *Rolling Stone* magazine) as 'The Greatest Unsigned Band in the World'. The group had honed their skills during the mid-1980s while busking on Dublin's Grafton Street as The Benzini Brothers. Founder members Liam O'Maonlai (vocals/piano) and Fiachna O'Braonain (guitar) were also fluent Irish speakers well versed in traditional song, a background that underpinned the evolving Flowers' sound, which incorporated *sean-nós* singing styles as well as tin whistles and bodhráns. But in truth this trad dimension was only ever a single texture in the band's eclectic fusion of rock, soul and blues forms.

Indeed, there was little evidence of the group's trad credentials on their soul-inflected debut single, 'Love Don't Work This Way', which was given an Irish-only release on U2's Mother label in 1987 after Bono had seen the band performing on *The Late Late Show*. A number of other Irish groups, most notably In Tua Nua and Cactus World News, had previously signed for the label, but with only modest commercial success. In common with these earlier acts, the Flowers were swiftly picked up by a major international label (London Records), and received something of a head start when they got the chance to perform their international debut single, 'Don't Go', for several million television viewers at the 1988 Eurovision Song Contest (held in Dublin after the competition had been won the previous year by easy-listening crooner Johnny Logan). The group made their appearance in the special-guest slot during voting intermission (a role famously filled by Bill Whelan's *Riverdance* extravaganza five years later), displaying a

Best Bit: The initial saxophone break during the first instrumental refrain at 1.14, briefly evoking lush vistas far beyond the narrow confines of the song's repetitive two-chord structure.

degree of 'authenticity' – as virtuouso multi-instrumentalists performing their own material on piano, saxophone and acoustic guitar – that sat rather incongruously with the high artifice of Eurovision. More significantly, it also went against the grain of the late 1980s pop landscape, which had been radically reconfigured by rap, hip hop and house music.

From a purely sartorial perspective, the group had less in common with western Europe in the 1980s than with the West Coast of America in the late 1960s. Making symbolic alliance with the nascent eco-consciousness of the period, the band's characteristic look – featuring long hair, ponchos, beads and sandals – offered a nouveau-hippy tonic to the increasing corporatism of the (pre-Celtic Tiger) Republic, as well as the hardening sectarianism north of the border (1988 was the year of the infamous Gibraltar shootings and the spiralling violence that ensued).

The band's penchant for warmth, sincerity and emotional honesty is very much in evidence on 'Don't Go', a mid-tempo but up-beat tune based on a simple two-chord trick (A–E). Opening with a gently strummed acoustic guitar and blues-inflected piano, O'Maonlai, whose highly resonant mid-register vocal is marked by a distinctly American-style enunciation, presents the listener with a series of snapshots of idyllic

1988

summer scenes. So, in the opening line, the singer notices 'a smell of fresh cut grass filling up my senses', while in the second verse he finds himself 'lying warm on soft sandy beaches', all of which serves to evoke an imaginary Edenic space that stands in stark contrast to the neo-realist portrait of the band's home town that emerged at this time in *The Commitments,* Roddy Doyle's fictional account of the Dublin music scene.

Later on, O'Maonlai's words take a quasi-hallucinagenic turn in what is effectively the track's middle eight at 1.36, when the singer – whose heavily reverberated vocal is temporarily foregrounded above all else in the mix – offers an almost evangelical spoken-sung testimony of an apparently visionary experience: 'There's white horses and they're coming at me at a pace / And there's a blue sirocco blowing warm into my face,' he recounts, before gesturing towards the supernatural by stressing the presence of 'a black cat lying in the shadow of a gatepost'.

In line with the track's distinctly feel-good sensibility, though, the black cat only serves to signify 'that love is on its way', and the song happily returns to its affirmative chorus in which the singer invites his addressee to 'stick around laugh a while'. Such chorus sections are bolstered by the band's multi-tracked high-register backing vocals and, in the final renditions, by a descending harmonica motif. Elsewhere, relief is provided by the track's subtle modulation at two key moments to an F#–F chord progression that facilitates Leo Barnes's brief but impressive saxophone flourishes.

Perhaps unsurprisingly – given the degree of exposure that the song received at Eurovision '88 – 'Don't Go' went on to achieve considerable success, with the single reaching No. 11 in the UK charts, and the band making a memorable appearance on *Top of the Pops.* However, although they went on to record two critically acclaimed and commercially successful albums, *People* (1988) and *Home* (1990), Hothouse Flowers – who continue to tour and record – have failed to produce a song to match the success of 'Don't Go'.

Arclight

THE FAT LADY SINGS [EAST WEST]

It was the year of perestroika, when the Soviet empire was rocked (in the non-musical sense) all across eastern Europe. November saw the beginning of the end of the Berlin Wall, while the crumbling of the Ceausescu regime in Romania over Christmas was watched with a mixture of fascination and trepidation. The world was being turned upside down, and it was all (as both the radicals and the reactionaries of the 1960s had predicted) on television.

In Ireland, also, new questions were beginning to make the old answers seem redundant. The Tiger was still just a cub but there were signs of economic growth and a fall-off in the emigration which had been such a blight throughout the 1980s. Although Mary Robinson wouldn't win her historic presidential victory until the following year, the winds of change were beginning to blow through Mallow as irresistibly as they were through Moscow.

The Fat Lady Sings were formed in 1986, a significant date in as much as it falls between two extremely active periods in Irish rock history: the A&R heaven that was Dublin in the early 1980s following U2's emergence as world contenders, and the hue and cry caused by Alan Parker's 1991 film of Roddy Doyle's *The Commitments*. FLS did not aspire to either the heroic tendencies of early U2 nor the blue-eyed, 'workin'-class' soul of the early 1990s. Rather, they were possessed of a distinctive rock voice, peculiar though not quirky, lacking gimmickry of any kind but immediately recognizable.

Musically, FLS were the classic 1980s rock unit, possessing an excellent guitarist in Tim Bradshaw and a tight rhythm section in Rob Hamilton (drums) and Dermot Lynch (bass). The band's ace, however, was always going to be front man Nick Kelly – in 1989, a young vocalist and songwriter in possession of charisma, looks and talent in roughly equal measures. Some guys, as Robert Palmer might have put it, have all the luck. Kelly also had a unique voice which was to become emblematic of the FLS sound. Powerful and breathy by turns, it was the perfect instrument with which to express the catchy, ambivalent lyrics he composed.

'Arclight' was FLS's third single, following 'Fear and Favour' (1986) and 'Be Still' (1988). The latter turned up along with 'Arclight' on the band's debut album, *Twist* (1991), by which time Kelly and Co. had signed to East West and relocated to London in pursuit of the mainstream success that inevitably eluded them at home. The band worked hard in the UK and US, but things were already looking unlikely by the time the main man famously pulled the plug in January 1994. This deed seemed vindicated a few years later by *Between Trapezes* (1997), a solo album that Kelly defiantly organized (including funding, recording and distribution) outside the rock music industry he had come to disdain.

When you look back at the songs written and sung by Kelly during his FLS days, you get the impression of a man too sensitive and too intelligent to survive the remorseless ones-and-zeros logic of the music industry. Here's a guy with a pop musician's sensibility for melody and structure but with a poet's gift for language. Unlike classic pop and rock, which attempts to express *something* – usually love or loss of love – Kelly's songs invariably describe *something* that may be *nothing*. The typical scenario he constructs is one in which love and loss are always provisional, conditional, radically unfinished. 'What's true tonight won't be true tomorrow morning', he sings on 'Broken Into', the opening track from *Twist*. Complex emotions such as these demand complex expression; tentative feelings require tentative language. Kelly's achievement was to marry very un-pop-like phrasing and sentiments with original pop melodies and production, and to be able to express both in terms of a vocal style that was simultaneously melodramatic and sincere.

Classic popular music discourse, in other words, is always in search of 'the answer'. This is not something we're going to find in 'Arclight', however. It *sounds* like a positive statement, with its resonant E major key and its brightly harmonized melody; but it's a song in which relations between the protagonist and their interlocutor are unresolved, and are likely to remain so. Both are 'lost', but both are wary of trying to compensate

. . . .

Best Bit: The five magnificent 'shine' similes of the chorus – rock lyrics are poetry (maybe).

. . . .

for loss with a new love, or of letting the mood that has emerged between them harden into anything that might have a name. The singer accepts that 'you've no answers', and is content. In this context, the 'arclight' image is particularly appropriate, for not only is it a thing *in* itself, it also serves to illuminate *other* things around it. Light is a catalyst for change in its immediate surroundings, producing shades and shadows (and thus meanings) that are independent of the source yet linked to it at the same time. Fire, likewise, is fundamental but destructive, bringing the warmth of love at one moment and the flames of obliteration at another. The light that 'shines' tonight may 'burn' tomorrow morning, and who is to say which is right or true?

What we have in this song, then, is the musical approximation of a mood, a moment, an attempt to approach one level of ineffable experience through the terms of another. This desire determines Kelly's use here of the traditional poetic figure of the simile. A

1989

simile, after all, brings together two things that we don't normally associate in everyday life, with the effect of making us look differently at both. When Robbie Burns wrote 'My love is like a red, red rose', he didn't mean that his girlfriend had petals and thorns and grew on a bush in the earth; he was drawing, rather, on a particular eighteenth-century conceit which connoted nature with innocence and freshness, but also with undertones of sorrow and mortality.

Just so in 'Arclight', which is awash with similes, some of them conventional ('shine in the morning like the sun, burn like a candle in the night'; 'I am as free as the air'), some of them startling in their originality ('shine like a book that's never been read, burn like a saint who knows that he's right'; 'I am as free as the old'). The former set up a context in which the bizarre couplings of the latter may be all the more fully appreciated. The song doesn't reach closure, the guy doesn't *get* the girl; the worlds of 'the thing' and that to which 'the thing' is likened are not pulled together in a final, resolving image. Rather, 'Arclight' fades out on an image – 'You burn me down', overlapped and harmonized – which unites salvation with destruction.

Disappointment awaits those who expect rock musicians to be able to answer the great questions of love and life; but we should expect them, no less than any artist, to find beautiful ways to ask such questions. 'Arclight' does just that.

1990

I Am Stretched on Your Grave

SINÉAD O'CONNOR [ENSIGN]

Irish rock music prior to the 1990s had been dominated by a series of male figures (from Van and Rory to Bono via Lynott and Geldof). Elsewhere, a range of critically acclaimed and commercially successful female artists had flourished since the 1960s, most notably in the UK (with the likes of Dusty Springfield, Kate Bush and Annie Lennox) and the US (Janis Joplin, Debbie Harry, Madonna and so on). Irish women had featured to some degree in the showband phenomenon, mostly as band-fronting singers such as Eileen Reid And The Cadets (whose 'I Gave My Wedding Dress Away' was a huge hit in 1964), Tina And The Mexicans and Kelley And The Nevada. Although not a part of the scene, the same showband ethos was tapped by Dana when she won the Eurovision Song Contest in 1970 with 'All Kinds of Everything'. There had also been a significant female dimension to the folk and trad boom, with performers such as Gay Woods, the Johnston sisters, and Clodagh Simmonds and Alison O'Donnell of Dublin cult band Mellow Candle. This tradition of female trad folkies continued into the 1970s and beyond with Clannad sisters Eithne and Máire Ní Bhraonáin, and numerous other artists amongst whom the most popular were Mary and Frances Black, Dolores Keane and Maura O'Connell.

It would be fair to say that most of these women were projecting fairly traditional images of Irish womanhood. Amongst all the lovely girls and earth mothers, there was little (with the possible exceptions of Galway blues-singer Mary Coughlan and Dublin punk outfit The Boy Scoutz) in the way of direct engagement with the real condition of contemporary femininity, Irish or otherwise. All this was to change, however, with Sinéad O'Connor's devastating entry onto the late 1980s pop landscape. Sporting a shaved head, bomber jacket and Doc Martens, Sinéad offered – on early singles 'Troy' (1987) and 'Mandinka' (1988) – an aggressive, angst-laden antidote to the established array of Irish female imagery, as well as to the bland 'girl next-door' formula of global pop starlets like Debbie Gibson and Tiffany. The fierce belligerence at the forefront of O'Connor's performances was always counterposed, however, by an extraordinarily

OOH, DEAR! I DON'T NO
YOURS MUCH

tender vocal style and a striking, wide-eyed vulnerability (hence the now famous caricature of the singer as 'a Bambi in bovver boots'). Such incongruity pointed less to the androgyny of pop convention, though, than to a far more complex set of paradoxes at the heart of Sinéad's character.

Born on the Catholic feast day of the Immaculate Conception and delivered by the son of Éamon de Valéra, the patriarch of modern Ireland, O'Connor had an emotionally fraught upbringing marked by the abusive behaviour of an alcoholic mother. Notwithstanding this early trauma, Sinéad – who was raised in relative prosperity in Glenageary, Co. Dublin – went on to study voice and piano at Dublin's College of Music, and by the early 1980s was collaborating with Dublin folk rockers In Tua Nua. The band's obvious preference for Leslie Dowdall, though, encouraged O'Connor to set up her own group, an acoustic/funk outfit called Ton Ton Macoute. Shortly thereafter, Sinéad was spotted by A&R reps from London's Ensign label (who effectively poached her with the offer of a solo deal), and sessions quickly began for what would eventually become her debut album, *The Lion and the Cobra* (1987).

Though this album was an unequivocal success in its own right, shifting one million copies and attracting a Grammy nomination, few could have anticipated the rapid ascent of Sinéad's star profile in 1990. The year began with the release of 'Nothing Compares 2 U', a cover of a relatively obscure Prince song originally penned for little-known Minneapolis band The Family. Accompanied by John Maybury's now iconic video in which a pale-skinned and polo-necked O'Connor is seen to produce an apparently genuine tear, the single became a major hit on both sides of the Atlantic. Its success was exceeded, however, by the singer's landmark second album, *I Do Not Want What I Haven't Got* (1990), which sold six million copies, holding the No. 1 spot in the US album chart for eight weeks and receiving no less than four Grammy nominations. In the process, Sinéad became Ireland's first female pop superstar and the only Irish artist of the era to pose a serious threat to the domestic hegemony of U2 (with whom she maintained a troubled relationship, despite collaborating with guitarist The Edge on his 1986 single, 'Heroine').

A collection of intensely personal songs, *I Do Not Want* introduced the reflective, autobiographical note that has played such an important part in Sinéad's subsequent career. This is clearly signalled by the album's artwork (a shadowy, serene pose in stark contrast to the brightly lit animated gestures of *The Lion and the Cobra*), as well as the singer's decision to open the album with a recitation of Reinhold Neibhurr's Serenity Prayer. The material itself, meanwhile, is marked by the confessional intimacy associated with the singer-songwriter tradition, as Sinéad trades the distorted barre chords of her debut for acoustic guitars and string arrangements in songs that are deceptively simple while containing many complex, multi-layered textures.

This desire to open up fresh terrain is strikingly evident on the album's second track, 'I Am Stretched on Your Grave'. Based on a twelfth-century Gaelic poem ('Tá Mé Sínte Ar Do Thuama'), in which a man expresses grief for his deceased female lover, the song was melodically arranged and set to music for Sinéad by Phillip King, a well-known figure from the Irish rock scene and a former member of folk-rock outfit Scullion.

'I Am Stretched' is launched by a looping, mid-paced hip-hop groove that anticipates the singer's later work with acts such as Bomb The Bass, Massive Attack and Moby. At the same time, this medieval keening poem is animated throughout by a characteristically haunting vocal performance that, in its phrasing and use of grace notes, suggests the *sean-nós* style of traditional Irish singing. Adapting to this ancient style with remarkable aplomb, the singer offers a highly sympathetic rendition of the lyric, while a sparse synth-

Best Bit: Steve Wickham's sixty-second fiddle solo in which the track's remarkable fusion of hip hop and trad is stunningly realized.

bass registers the root notes of key chords. The track's percussive shuffle, meanwhile, is punctuated throughout by a reverberating snare and simulated 'scratching' that bestow it with a contemporary edge. This splicing of ostensibly incongruous styles may have initially taken listeners by surprise, but the track is undoubtedly successful in its daring fusion of techno and trad, not least during the remarkable fiddle solo with which it ends.

If this weaving of contemporary and traditional styles was 'very much the product', as the late *Hot Press* writer Bill Graham put it, 'of a London exile', the song's highly effective blending of seemingly disparate impulses was also symptomatic of Sinéad's frequently paradoxical character. Indeed, this particular track is marked throughout by incongruity. For instance, while the lyrics describe an intensely emotional commitment of supernatural proportions (owing more to pre-modern poetry than postmodern pop), they also evoke adolescent desires more typical of the genre ('When my family thinks that I'm safe in my bed …'). Similarly, while the song's narrator genuflects to Catholic codes on pre-marital sex ('Thanks be to Jesus we did what was right / And your maidenhead still is your pillar of light'), the sheer intensity of the enduring relationship nevertheless offends Church protocol ('The priests and the friars approach me in dread / Because I still love you my love and you're dead').

Sinéad herself went on, of course, to develop a particularly fractious relationship with the Catholic Church, most notably when she shredded a photograph of the Pope during a live television performance in the US in 1992. Notwithstanding the obvious myth-making potential of such controversies, the singer's attacks on the Church – in tandem with her revelations of child abuse, abortion and her parents' divorce – served to illuminate aspects of Irish society often rendered invisible in official accounts of the nation. Such issues, which formed centre-stage debates in late twentieth-century Ireland, were in many ways crystallized in the persona of Sinéad, who later became a priest herself. God only knows what Dev would've made of it all.

1991

Soon

MY BLOODY VALENTINE [CREATION]

Tuesday, 15 July 2003. It finally came, the news that so many within the rock music world had been waiting for: 'My Bloody Valentine Return to Studio to Complete Unfinished Album'. After a dozen years, during which they were lionized as one of the most important and original rock voices ever to appear on the right side of the Atlantic, three members of the classic line-up – Kevin Shields, Colm O'Ciosiog and Bilinda Butcher (no sign of bass-player Debbie Googe) – were apparently holed up in a Berlin studio working on a number of tracks that had been abandoned during the sessions for 1989's *Glider* EP. The questions proliferated: Could it be true? *New* (as opposed to bootlegged or remixed, or God save us, *covered*) My Bloody Valentine material? Where had they been? What had they been doing? Would advances in recording and instrumental technology change the band's sound? Had Kevin washed his hair?

MBV had spent the 1990s as one of the world's most 'influential' bands, name-checked (and what a good name it is) by the hip (Billy Corgan), the unhip (The Edge) and ... eh ... Noel Gallagher. They never officially broke up, but as the months and then years went by there was a widespread sense that the world had heard the last of the Anglo-Irish quartet. A forlorn message on one of the websites dedicated to the band – abandoned like the Marie Celeste itself – still reads 'Last updated January 17, 1995'.

Shields (born in New York but raised in Dublin) and O'Ciosiog and some other guys formed the bones of MBV in Dublin in 1984. With a name taken from a Canadian horror flick, the fledgling band demonstrated anti-mainstream tendencies from the outset. Feeling unappreciated at home, MBV Mark I took off for Germany where they recorded the ultra-rare mini-album entitled *This Is Your Bloody Valentine* (1985). All European rock roads lead to London, however, and that was where the band fetched up in 1985. The call for Live Aid not forthcoming, MBV pressed on regardless, recording a number of singles and EPs for different indie labels, and bringing onboard Googe on bass and Butcher on guitar-and-vocals(ish). This was the period during which MBV began to establish their characteristic sound, and to display a disdain for personal and domestic hygiene that would make 'scruffy' Bob Geldof look like a well-groomed yuppie.

My Bloody Valentine were picked up by Creation boss Alan McGee after they supported his own band Biff Bang Pow! somewhere in Kent on a cold night in January 1988. Extremely impressed, and with The Jesus And Mary Chain on sabbatical and The House Of Love no longer his main concern (having moved on to Fontana for a record fee), McGee began to tout MBV as the Next Big Indie Thing, which is not quite the same as the Next Big Thing but quite good all the same. Creation had emerged in the early 1980s as part of the British post-punk 'indie' revolution – ideologically, musically and much of the time personally opposed to the major labels and their corporate approach to the rock 'business'. One of the things about indie popular music, however, was that it wasn't very popular, and in order to reach any kind of audience beyond a few thousand die-hard purists around the country both the labels and the artists were forced sooner or later to get into bed with the major label enemy. During the course of the 1980s Creation – along with Factory and Rough Trade – came to exemplify not only the flawed idealism of the indie movement, but also the pragmatism and sheer bloody-mindedness it would need to survive.

McGee's faith in MBV seemed vindicated by the string of releases they produced throughout 1988, culminating in November's well-received *Isn't Anything* album. Shields was being depicted in British indie circles as another eccentric genius possessed of both a unique rock 'vision', and the talent and determination to realize it. Already, however, he and the rest of MBV had begin to show signs of the ... let's be generous and call it 'fastidiousness', that was to characterize their studio work from now on. Not quite in the Lee Mavers (of The La's) class, Shields and the gang were nonetheless fully committed to capturing the sounds they heard in their heads, and had few scruples about spending

....

Best Bit: The rhythm track which kicks in after 8 seconds, inviting all those indie kids to leave the bar and get out on the floor. If only we'd listened.

....

Mr McGee's money in pursuit of those sounds. And so *Glider* was cut from a proposed album to a four-track EP, and was the band's only release during 1990 after a completely blank 1989. Another four-track EP, *Tremolo,* appeared in February 1991, before finally, nineteen studios, thousands of pounds and very nearly one bankrupt record label later, the album *Loveless* appeared in November of 1991.

My Bloody Valentine are famous for instigating the 'shoe-gazing' school of British rock, practised in their wake by the likes of Ride, Lush and Chapterhouse. The moniker arose in the first instance from the penchant of these artists to gaze at their footwear during performance rather than interact with the audience in any kind of traditional way. You'd never hear Rachel of Slowdive, for instance, saying: 'Good evening, Dunstable – are you ready to *rock*?!' But 'shoe-gazing' also came to connote a specific set of musical associations, and again, MBV were the prime instigators here. Over the years, their sound had mutated from a kind of sub-Mary Chain punk into something else altogether – a wall of shrieking, moaning, wailing guitars around which floated a variety of dissonant textures, including percussion, strings and vocals. Their achievement was to take the Reid brothers' 'revolutionary' early sound – produced by an uncertain blend of (in no particular order) drunkenness, laziness and ineptitude – and invest it with melody and structure. The result was a kind of music that was extremely 'noisy' (MBV concerts were notoriously bad for your hearing – some have speculated that damaged eardrums was in fact the reason for the band's disappearance), yet seemed capable of great beauty and emotion at the same time.

'Soon' first appeared on the *Glider* EP, resurfacing two years later as the last and longest track on *Loveless*. Besides the characteristically dense guitar sound and the usual indiscernible vocals, it also features a trippy synth loop and – surprise, surprise – a rhythm you can dance to. As such, 'Soon' was obviously influenced by the revolution that had been developing on the British underground music scene since the late 1980s: the fusion of acid house and indie. Beginning with the Manchester bands The Happy Mondays and The Stone Roses, this dance floor/guitar crossover had received perhaps its definitive statement in an album released in September 1991 by MBV's Creation label-mates Primal Scream: the Mercury Prize-winning *Screamadelica*. However, MBV's star was to be eclipsed – at least in terms of mainstream success – not by Bobby Gillespie and crew, but by another album from September 1991: *Nevermind* by Seattle grunge rockers Nirvana. In this regard, it's worthwhile considering what would have happened to popular music in the years since 1991 if 'Soon' rather than 'Smells Like Teen Spirit' had been pushed by the international taste-makers who regulate what 'the kids' get to hear. True, we probably wouldn't have had the phenomenon of American neo-punk, but would that really have been such a bad thing?

1992

Dreams

THE CRANBERRIES [ISLAND]

By the early 1990s, a number of provincial Irish bands had made their mark on the country's rock scene. However, not since the heyday of Granny's Intentions at the back end of the 1960s had any band from Limerick (the Republic's third major city) made any significant impression. With the exception of Denis Allen's dire tribute to the Treaty City, 'Limerick, You're a Lady' (1979), the only recent act to make a serious impact on the national scene had been 1980s outfit Tuesday Blue. The city's marginal position on Ireland's rock map would change dramatically in the 1990s, however, when The Cranberries became Limerick's best-known export since Richard Harris, temporarily eclipsing even U2 in the global rock arena.

Formed as a college indie act in 1989 – initially under the moniker The Cranberry Saw Us – the band was based around guitar-playing brothers Noel and Mike Hogan (lead and bass respectively) and drummer Fergal Lawler. When original vocalist Niall Quinn decided to leave the group in 1990, an unknown teenage girl, Dolores O'Riordan, successfully auditioned as his replacement. A trained pianist raised on traditional and church songs in rural Ballybricken, O'Riordan immediately began writing new material with guitarist Noel, launching a songwriting partnership that has persisted throughout the group's career.

With Dolores at the forefront of the newly renamed Cranberries, the band put together a series of live dates and demo tapes, culminating in the release of a four-track EP, *Uncertain,* on the local Xeric label in October 1991. The record generated a considerable buzz amongst London A&R types, sparking a bidding war that was eventually won by Island. Sessions immediately began for the group's debut album, *Everybody Else Is Doing It So Why Can't We?* (1993), which displayed an unmistakably 'indie' aesthetic (jangly guitars, fey vocals, introspective lyrics), owing an especially obvious debt to Irish-Mancunians The Smiths. In fact, ex-Smiths producer Stephen Street was flown in to oversee the project, while Morrissey's former Rough Trade boss, Geoff Travis, took on managerial responsibilities.

Everybody Else was much more than an 'indie' tribute album, though, for the band's freshly polished sound had a warmth and a vibrancy that was very much their own. Moreover, the prolific Hogan-O'Riordan partnership had furnished the group with a plethora of top-quality tunes. Nowhere is this stunning blend of lush textures, fine songwriting (and 'indie'-fixated guitar playing) more evident than on the group's international debut single, 'Dreams' (1992).

Set in motion by a suite of crashing power chords, the track has an immediate epic sweep, its multi-layered textures and subtle synth-tones pointing to Street's meticulous production. Meanwhile, a remarkably tight rhythm section punctuates the song's simple chord changes (E–A–B7), before the band shift seamlessly into the low-key opening verse. Here, Hogan switches to a gently picked arpeggio of open and fretted strings, underpinned by his brother's punchy bass line and Lawler's understated drumming. None of this anticipates the breathless fragility of O'Riordan's vocal, her high-register delivery powerfully evoking the song's adolescent ache: 'Oh my life / Is changing everyday / In every possible way.'

Undoubtedly the most affecting texture in the track's mosaic, O'Riordan's double-tracked vocals counter-harmonize throughout, showcasing the singer's audibly Irish accent. Expertly accompanied by Lawler's reverberated drumming – recalling Joy Division's awe-inspiring 'Atmosphere' (1979) – a couple of heavily choused open chords pick up the song's original tempo. This eventually leads to an abrupt and relatively shapeless middle eight (G–C), with O'Riordan's startling falsetto of non-linguistic sounds ('La …') evoking the subconscious world of the song's title.

Recovering from this slow-paced fragment, the track returns to its central figure, but only for O'Riordan's voice to become increasingly urgent ('And now I tell you openly / You have my heart so don't hurt me'). Respite is eventually offered when the band restore the relative tranquillity of the opening verse, but this merely serves as preface to the song's lengthy coda, an unrestrained rendition of the track's intro set against Dolores' vocal acrobatics. Picking up where she left off in the middle eight, the singer is

Best Bit: The enchanting intro with its clean, simple lines full of youthful promise and wonder – no wonder the Irish Tourist Board nabbed it for a TV commercial in the UK.

now accompanied by a mid-register counter-melody, provided by Mike Mahoney. The band had evidently been listening to a lot of world music, especially Peter Gabriel's *Passion* (1989), and this closing duet conjures an unmistakably North African vocal style.

A remarkably ambitious debut effort, 'Dreams' was lauded as 'Single of the Week' in *Melody Maker*, but made little mark on the UK charts. *Everybody Else* fared little better, getting stuck at a lowly No. 64. Many critics saw the band as an Irish simulation of English indie outfit The Sundays, while others made unfavourable comparisons between Dolores and another feisty, short-haired, Irish female singer.

A crucial turning point in the group's career came, however, when they secured a high-profile support slot on Suede's North American tour in late 1993. The Cranberries' second single, 'Linger' (1993), had just been picked up for heavy rotation on US MTV, and American fans of the Limerick group started voting with their feet, walking out of Suede shows before the headline act had even hit the stage. As the single gradually made its way into the US Top Ten, the band – who had effectively by-passed the usual industry gatekeepers in London and Dublin – finally began to be taken seriously at home.

The City of Limerick took the unprecedented step of holding a civic reception in the group's honour, while Dublin's *Hot Press* granted the band their first cover story. By this stage, *Everybody Else* was scaling the charts on both sides of the Atlantic, reaching the No. 1 spot in the UK a full twelve months after its original release. Even 'Dreams', the group's relaunched debut single, achieved hit status in the summer of 1994, with the band celebrating in front of 100,000 fans at 'Woodstock II' as their album shifted upwards of seven million copies.

The belated success of *Everybody Else* meant that the group's new-found fan base had little time to assimilate 'Dreams' before they were subjected to the band's next effort, 'Zombie' (1994). The record marked a distinct shift in musical style, abandoning indie feyness for grungy aggression, and swapping adolescent narcissism for a highly polemical evocation of the Troubles. Bizarrely, the release of the single coincided with the emergent Peace Process in Northern Ireland, and many critics saw its Troubles theme as a cynical marketing ploy (despite the fact that the record's release date had been scheduled for several months). In any case, 'Zombie' proved extremely popular with the group's fans, shifting two million copies worldwide, while its host album, *No Need to Argue* (1994), sold an astonishing sixteen million.

By the mid-1990s, however, the musical landscape – particularly in the UK and Europe – was beginning to shift after the preliminary tremors of Britpop. In stark contrast to the likes of Blur and Oasis, though, The Cranberries had already 'broken' in the US, and the band strove to consolidate their North American profile by recruiting Canadian soft-metal producer Bruce Fairburn to oversee their poorly conceived third collection, *To the Faithful Departed* (1996). Though the album sold well, it was critically derided, and a punishing promotional schedule began to take its toll on the group. Things came to a head when an increasingly emaciated O'Riordan – and her visibly fatigued band mates – were forced to cancel a major US tour. Subsequent efforts *Bury the Hatchet* (1999) and *Wake Up and Smell the Coffee* (2001) left much to be desired, and after an obligatory 'best of' set, *Stars* (2002), the group parted company with Island Records. Though still playing live to adoring audiences across the globe, The Cranberries have rarely fulfilled the promise set by their perfect-pop debut.

N17 (live)

THE SAW DOCTORS [SOLID]

The small cathedral town of Tuam, Co. Galway boasts few rock 'n' roll credentials. In fact, at the turn of the 1990s, its only legitimate claim to rock history was that Johnny Rotten's father had been born there. Rotten had of course made his name in the late 1970s punk scene, before turning to experimental dub-reggae with PiL. It was particularly fitting, then, that Tuam's first major rock outfit, The Saw Doctors, should emerge from the ashes of various punk and reggae acts in the town.

The Saw Doctors first came together in 1987, when guitarist Davy Carton (formerly of Tuam punk outfit Blaze X) joined forces with singer/guitarist Leo Moran of local reggae act Too Much For The White Man. After a formative show at Tuam's Imperial Hotel, the pair experimented with a series of line-up changes before settling on Pearse Doherty (bass, tin whistle), John Donnelly (drums) and multi-instrumentalist John 'Turps' Burke.

Taking their name from Irish travelling folk who sharpened old saws for a living, the band's sound was an eclectic fusion of country, trad, folk and rock (famously described by *Mojo* magazine as 'punko-Nashville-folk-rock'). Meanwhile, their lyrical concerns were unashamedly provincial, focusing on the everyday features of small-town Irish life (Christian Brothers, Gaelic games, convent girls). The tone of this material was invariably one of earthy humour, a trait that marked the band's earliest endeavours, not least *Crackle and Buzz*, a *Rattle and Hum* parody film shot at Galway's Claddagh Palace cinema.

With their plain clothes and ordinary looks, The Saw Doctors were often derided as an unfortunate throwback, representing an insular, retrogressive Ireland at a time of postmodern change (the infant Celtic Tiger was just starting to purr). These criticisms weren't unfounded, but the band's sound was pioneering in its own right, fusing the folk and showband ethos of agrarian east Galway with a transnational rock aesthetic. As Carton memorably put it, 'our ambition is to bring the lounge-bar atmosphere of the west of Ireland to the world stage'.

This was no mean feat, and one for which the group would eventually be honoured as Free Men of Tuam. However, it's worth pointing out that they received some fairly high-profile support along the way. Back in 1988, Waterboy Mike Scott – temporarily based in Galway for the legendary *Fisherman's Blues* sessions – had witnessed an early Saw Doctors show at the city's Quays Pub, where the band had a six-week residency. Shortly thereafter, Scott invited the group to support The Waterboys on their UK and Irish tour, whilst also producing debut single, 'N17' (1989).

Elevating the road to Shannon Airport as a kind of Irish 'Route 66', the song remains one of the most affecting accounts of Irish emigration ever composed. Nevertheless, it initially met with very little success, selling only a handful of copies. Undeterred, the group turned their attention to an old Blaze X song, 'I Used to Love Her'. Reworked and retitled, 'I Useta Love Her' (1990) went straight to No. 1 in Ireland, where it remained for an unprecedented nine weeks, becoming the country's best selling single of all time. By Christmas it had been joined in the Top Five by a reissued 'N17' (1990), before the latter was given a major international launch – alongside debut album *If This Is Rock and Roll I Want My Old Job Back* – in 1991.

By this stage, the band had become a major live draw in Ireland, making memorable appearances at the 'Feile' gig in Thurles, as well as the famous 'West's Awake' event in Tuam (alongside Mike Scott and The Hothouse Flowers). What might be termed 'The Year of The Saw Doctors' culminated in a New Year's Eve show for 8,000 fans at Dublin's

··

Best Bit: 'And as we turned left at Claregalway, I could feel a lump in my throat' – a line that could reduce one of McAlpine's Fusiliers to tears.

··

Point. Over the next decade, Tuam's favourite sons became a live staple at festivals across the UK (Glastonbury, Cambridge, the Fleadh) and Europe (not to mention Australia and the US). It was indeed as a live prospect that the group really flourished, although the precise attraction of their music for international rock audiences remains unclear: what makes a song such as 'N17' such a perennial live favourite in places as diverse as Stockholm and Sydney, Norwich and New York?

The track is launched by a cheery accordion motif, its ascending, upbeat tenor matched by a subtle mandolin riff, simple acoustic guitar (G–C) and solid rhythm section. Moran's vocal is characteristically precise, its unadorned quality drawing attention to a lyric which found its way onto the Irish Leaving Cert syllabus. It's not difficult to see why, as the words manage to evoke – with effortless poignancy and remarkable concision – the social experience of millions of Irish people since the 1950s, including unemployment, religion and emigration (and that's just the opening couplet).

Leaving Tuam for an unspecified 'foreign soil' (it could be the UK, the US or Australia), the song's narrator finds himself 'reminiscing' about 'the prefabs' and his 'old friends'. However, in stark contrast to the naive sentimentality often associated with Ireland's diaspora, this migrant keenly recognizes that his hometown will not be preserved in aspic ('I know that things would be different / If I ever decide to go back').

And while the song's chorus is unashamedly homesick ('I wish I was on that N17'), there is nothing maudlin about Moran's belting vocals, his Springsteen-esque delivery underpinned by a robust chord change (G–Em–D) and C&W guitar lick. Meanwhile, the collectively sung chorus hook ('stone walls and the grasses green') offers a defiantly upbeat riposte to the exile's experience, offsetting the pain of nostalgia with a jovial communality. A reflective moment is nevertheless permitted in the downbeat third verse (that effectively serves as the song's middle eight). Here, the kernel of the song's meaning is revealed through a series of stark contrasts, between 'filthy overcrowded trains' and twisty Galway roads, setting the 'muddled up problems / Of living on a foreign soil' against the assumed simplicity of traditional Irish life.

There is of course a much less negative way of thinking about emigration (as possibility, prospect and opportunity), as well as a far more dystopian take on rural Ireland (as narrow, parochial and lifeless). However, in all migrant experiences there is the emotional pull of 'home', and this is what The Saw Doctors captured so effectively in 'N17'. One can only assume that their legions of non-Irish fans have found some kind of universal resonance in the song's folkish simplicity. Whether or not this is the case, 'N17' has had little chart success outside Ireland, although the group did secure a string of hit singles in the UK in the mid-1990s with 'Small Bit of Love' (1994), 'World of Good' (1996) and 'To Win Just Once' (1996). Benefiting from their numerous appearances on *Top of the Pops,* the group's third album *Same Old Town* (1996) reached No. 6 in the UK chart. By this stage, they had launched their own record label, Shamtown ('sham' being traveller-speak for Tuam-dweller). However, it has been in the live – rather than the recorded – arena that the group have secured their reputation as leading purveyors of 'craic', transporting the bar-room vibes of east Galway to innumerable rock venues around the globe. Nothing insular about that.

1994

Goodbye Charlie Moonhead

ASLAN [BMG]

Okay, Mr Parker, here's the pitch: five young working-class Dubliners from the city's northside impress lots of people during the 1980s with their classic guitar-oriented rock music. They make an excellent debut album full of great tunes and tight performances. Then their charismatic lead singer implodes under the pressure of his drug addiction, and the rest of the band – no angels themselves – chuck him out. *He* recovers and starts again in a new set-up; *they* plod on in various formats, but the magic is missing for all parties. Five years on from the break-up, the estranged members reconcile for a one-off charity gig on their home patch in Finglas, only to discover during rehearsals that they still love each other, and they begin to make beautiful music again. The come-back album is a brilliant statement on the turmoil of the previous years. More records follow throughout the 1990s, and although mainstream international success eludes them, the band find that they have developed an appeal – especially in live performance – for new generations who were barely twinkles in their mammies' eyes when the band first formed. Meanwhile, the country in which the band lives has been going through a death-and-rebirth thing which more or less parallels that of the band. Think of the cinematic symbolism you could develop – grainy footage of urban decay in the early part, claustrophobic and constrained, slowly giving way to bright shots full of colour and movement and conviction! What do you think, Mr Parker, can you picture it? What do you mean it's been done? Alright, I'm going, I'm going; but I can't help thinking you're missing out on a great opportunity here. Do you have Mr Scorsese's number?

Probably no one will ever make a film of Aslan's story, but somebody should. For one thing, it could serve future generations as documentary evidence of one of the classic rock 'n' roll narratives: adolescents discover love of rock music in tough neighbourhood; band forms with eyes on the prize; band disintegrates while awaiting glory after early promise; band rediscovers rock 'n' roll and reforms; band achieves and maintains local success. Aslan's career is testament to the fact that for most rock bands the music (as Sting once rather disingenuously put it) has to be its own reward, and that after the booze, the drugs, the expectation and exploitation, the hype and bitterness, there's always the possibility that you'll remember your love of the music, and why you wanted to be in a rock band in the first place. Aslan came back from the dead on the strength of that love and that memory, and it's the band's realization of this miracle, as much as the songs they write and sing, that constitutes their enduring appeal as an Irish pop-culture institution.

At the same time as they partake of this classic rock 'n' roll story, moreover, Aslan also exemplify certain aspects of modern Irish history in as much as the band's dual career straddles pre- and post-Celtic Tiger Ireland. Aslan formed in the early 1980s during one of the bleakest periods in the island's modern history – attrition in the north, recession in the south, and emigration the thought in everyone's mind. If Roddy Doyle's *The Commitments* (1987) is the comic vision that has endured, Dermot Bolger's early work – including the poetry collection *Finglas Lives* (1980), the novel *Night Shift* (1985) and the play *The Lament for Arthur Cleary* (1989) – encapsulates much more accurately for many people a sense of the bleakness of working-class life on Dublin's northside at this time with its seemingly endless cycle of poverty, brutality and limited opportunities – 'Everybody hits you', as Aslan's debut single 'This Is' puts it, 'everybody knocks you down'. This was indeed the milieu from which the five group members emerged, and their early music is indelibly shaped by that experience. Lead vocalist and front man Christy Dignam was perhaps the chief victim; tabloid rumours of his heroin-related death after the release of Aslan's debut album *Feel No Shame* (1988) were exaggerated, but it's almost as if the band did indeed have to die in some form or other before they could be reborn into the brighter days of the 1990s.

The release of *Goodbye Charlie Moonhead* the album coincided with the revival of Ireland's economic fortunes, which is now routinely dated to the upsurge in American investment that began in 1994. A rock 'n' roll narrative, in other words, overlapped and cross-fertilized with a national-economic narrative, each feeding and sustaining the other. That said, it's an album that looks back to the mire from which both band and country had just emerged rather than forward to the vibrant Hibernian metropolis populated by a generation of international bright young things.

'Madness', as both theme and motif, had been an important factor in Aslan's music from the outset of their career, and on this album it achieves emblematic status. The mood had been presaged by 1993's 'Crazy World', a comeback single (written during rehearsals for the Finglas charity event) that re-established the band in the country's popular consciousness. It's there again on tracks such as 'Games' ('It's so strange what's running round inside my head'), 'Sweet Time' ('If I had time to get my head together'), 'Maybe I'm Obsessed' ('She said I was insane today'), 'This Time' ('Drawing faces in a padded room'), and 'She Said So' ('I don't know what I see in her crazy eyes'). *Goodbye Charlie Moonhead* is in fact a survivor's handbook, with the 'I' persona trying to make sense of the madness from which he has barely escaped with his life. Sometimes (as in the titles just mentioned), he's back there in the middle of it all; sometimes he's just looking back with a mixture of relief and regret.

Best Bit: The gorgeous acoustic guitar that plays around the chorus which, in its delicate, tripping descent, perfectly captures the mood of wistfulness and release broached in the lyric.

The title track is neither one of the belt-'em-out ballads nor one of the rockier, riff-based numbers which formed the basis of Aslan's subsequent appeal as a live act. On an album of strong melodic perspectives, it's a muted, melancholic piece distinguished by a striking chorus (beginning 'All I have is everything …') in which beautifully understated harmonies are set against sympathetic instrumentation and an unexpected key change. Thematically, we're back in the crazy, smashed-out-of-your-brain world in which Christy had lived for much of the 1980s, a world in which local small-time 'mary jane' deals segued day by day into a hardcore habit (even if his preferred poison was smack rather than charlie). 'This couldn't last forever' is a statement that has to be earned if it's to have any moral force; the thing about Aslan (as any one of their fiercely loyal fans could tell you) is that they have indeed earned the right to make such statements.

Encapsulating the indolent, dangerous world of 1980s Dublin, 'Goodbye Charlie Moonhead' is the band's valediction to the youthful convictions that nearly claimed them. It's also the sound of the generation that lived to tell the tale, counting the cost of the past before they begin the task of fashioning the future.

We Don't Need Nobody Else

WHIPPING BOY [COLUMBIA]

A group of five friends came together some time during 1988 to play at the twenty-first-birthday party of an acquaintance in Edenderry, Co. Offaly. They called themselves Lolita and the Whipping Boy, and it must have been some party: instead of 'Wake Me Up Before You Go-Go' and 'Come On Eileen' they opted to cover material by the likes of The Fall and The Velvet Underground, thus offering an early hint of their future direction. The 'Lolita' bit was ditched when the band's female guitarist departed after finding God and failing to convert the other members.

Thereafter things became a bit more intense, and (The) Whipping Boy began to build a reputation as a 'difficult' band in more than one sense. The music itself was often compared with 'challenging' noiseniks such as My Bloody Valentine and Sonic Youth, while their gigs frequently had to be decided on points, with front man Ferghal McKee willing to go to extreme lengths (including self-harm) to keep it all real and to elicit what he considered to be an appropriate response from the audience. Two EPs for a British indie label were followed by a promising but otherwise unremarkable debut album entitled *Submarine* in 1992. Hopes were high, however, when the band got a deal with Sony subsidiary Columbia and recruited Warne Livesey (The The, Julian Cope) to produce what was intended to be their breakthrough album.

The result was *Heartworm*, as dark and dysfunctional an album as ever produced by an Irish rock band. The music on this challenging recording vacillates between subtlety (including the occasional use of strings, as on 'Morning Rise') and guitar-driven muscularity, while McKee's voice – a rich baritone which much of the time hovers around the border between speech and song – gives the material an aura of intimacy that is by turns enigmatic and unsettling. In all these respects, the album's signature track is the 'bonus' one with which it closes: 'A Natural'. The song's persona coolly describes the acute paranoid schizophrenia from which he claims to be suffering, and tracks its onset in terms of failed relationships with both his mother and his girlfriend. In some ways, in fact, the central theme of the album is the inability of men and women to understand each other. The music of 'A Natural', meanwhile, moves from sensitive reflection at the outset (featuring what sounds like an oboe) to atonal thrashing at the end, thus reflecting the conflict between the protagonist's incompatible 'selves'.

'We Don't Need Nobody Else' was the second of three singles (after 'Twinkle' and before 'When We Were Young') culled from *Heartworm*. The track begins in a rather low key manner, offering little sense of the drama that is to come – 'low-key' in the sense that the music is restrained and uncertain, but also in the sense that the F major in which it is performed is fairly unusual in the rock idiom. Even with a capo, F is not a particularly sympathetic key for the guitar (the mainstay of rock 'n' roll since Chuck Berry and Buddy Holly), while at the same time it falls outside the natural range of most rock vocalists. U2's Bono, for example, is possessed of an extremely high range for a tenor. The force and clarity he is able to achieve with his soaring vocals has always been a key element of the band's sound. It was only when U2 became self-conscious that Bono began on a regular basis to contort his voice downwards (the breathy 'spoken' verses of 'The Fly' from *Achtung Baby* (1991), for example) or upwards (the 'fat lady' falsetto on the bridge of the same track); even then, these were obviously 'ironic' perversions of Bono's 'real' voice, which was in any case always somewhere in the background overseeing events and waiting to emerge with the 'true' perspective on events.

Giving over so much of an analysis of Whipping Boy (and especially of this particular song) to Bono is ironic, for the great man is name-checked early in the lyric as one of the 'bodies' that 'we' don't need. Even by 1995, Irish artists had been bemoaning U2's pervasive influence for at least a decade, so there was not much shock or controversy value in the allusion. It's clear, however, that the disdain articulated in 'We Don't Need Nobody Else' goes much deeper than mere envy or begrudgery, and encompasses much more than the country's premier rock presence. The persona of this drama – like that of all the songs on *Heartworm* – is beyond such 'normal' considerations; or rather, he has tapped into a vein of gothic dismay that, apparently, underlies 'normal' Irish life.

The distance between Whipping Boy and 'normal' Ireland could be measured in terms of the controversy that arose around the description of domestic violence in the second verse. Some, simply identifying McKee with the male persona who admits to striking his partner for the first time during their relationship, accused the band of outright misogyny. (Interestingly, there was far less bother when Liam O'Maonlai, from the altogether sunnier Hothouse Flowers, confessed to 'pushing her round' in 'I'm Sorry' from 1988.) Others, slightly more sophisticated, regretted the invocation of domestic violence in such a context, as if the rock iconography with which it was suffused conferred glamour on behaviour that is categorically reprehensible. A few noted that the issue of male-on-female violence had suddenly risen to the top of a number of agenda, and was being discussed in places and by people not normally given to that sort of thing. Surely this was a good thing. It may have been out of kilter with the 'Ireland of the Welcomes', with lines of bouncing *Riverdance* babes, record economic growth and the three-car family; but if it was the truth, why weren't people – or at least more people – talking about it? If hitting our 'loved ones' is a part of everyday Irish life, was it not valid to introduce it as part of an everyday Irish story?

And what of the title – how come 'we don't need nobody else'? Is it because 'we' are proud and independent, disdaining the society into which we've been born with its Bonograph of success? Because we're emotionally crippled, incapable of the negotiations and compromises required to survive modern life? Because we're culturally disenfranchised? Poor? Insane? Or is it because the 'I' of the song is an evil, jealous

Best Bit: Paul Page's crashing guitar at the beginning of the first chorus – the first indication of the seething volcano of menace which lies beneath McKee's slacker persona.

bastard who's not going to allow 'his' woman out into public where she can ogle, and be ogled by, any passing prick? The persona of 'We Don't Need Nobody Else' is complex and volatile; he wouldn't be much fun to have a drink with, and you'd certainly want to think twice before accepting an invitation to set up home with him. But there he is, nevertheless – sulking around the dim flat, a brooding, lonely, menacing presence who refuses either to be silenced or to play the game.

If critical respect determined success in the music industry Whipping Boy would have been huge, but it doesn't, and they aren't. Even if differences – internal artistic ones, and external contractual ones – hadn't put paid to the band towards the end of the decade, their dark energy didn't sit at all well with Celtic Tiger Ireland and its smug, self-congratulatory culture. Whipping Boy's legacy is one major album which testifies to a willingness of at least some Irish people to face up to the ghosts – whether banal, comic or horrific – haunting modern Irish life.

1996

Revelate

THE FRAMES [ZTT]

The music of The Frames has run like an artery through Irish rock since the band was formed by Dubliner Glen Hansard in the early 1990s, bringing health and vigour back to a thirty-something body that was beginning to show its age. In an industry characterized by increasing specialization and the gradual superseding of a communicative rationale by an instrumental one, The Frames offered a beacon of independent light for all those Irish music-makers not pretty, pushy or poxy enough to impress the powers that be. Drawing on numerous influences and inspirations, the music of The Frames – which is passionate, guitar-based and song-oriented – could perhaps best be described as a special kind of soul music: Irish soul, or – with reference to the most immediate environment of the band's evolution – Dublin soul.

That Hansard should be responsible for producing such music is, of course, somewhat ironic given his role as Outspan Foster in Alan Parker's *The Commitments*, the highly successful film about a fictional Dublin soul group based on Roddy Doyle's novel of the same name. Whereas *The Commitments* merely sampled the authenticity of an African-American cultural tradition, however, The Frames were more concerned to produce what they considered to be an authentic popular-musical response to the times and places in which they had fetched up. It was the difference, once again, between the showband and the rock group – between music primarily tending towards, on the one hand, an industrial-entertainment ethos and, on the other, towards an artistic-romantic ethos. Andrew Strong (Deco Cuffe in *The Commitments*) may have a voice that belonged to God, but it was Hansard who went on to inspire belief and devotion amongst Ireland's rock music-loving populace. This is because the latter young Dubliner wrote and sang from the outset as if his life, rather than his career, depended on it, which in some senses it clearly did.

Hansard left school at an early age with the sole intention of writing and performing his own music. With support from his mother, he

made a demo, one copy of which ended up on the desk of an Island Records executive. The label was interested, and asked him to put a band together. Thus The Frames DC was born, named for the bicycle frames with which Hansard used to fill the garden of his Dublin home as a child. Some critics have claimed that The Frames have in fact always been Hansard plus a more or less transitory and/or creatively quiescent pool of players recruited to support his discrete musical vision, a contention that the band have vociferously denied from the beginning. Hansard is certainly the driving force behind The Frames, however; while others have come and gone, it's difficult to imagine the band continuing without their talisman and creative focus.

The Frames' first EP, *Turn On Your Record Player,* was released in 1990, followed the next year by a debut album entitled *Another Love Song.* The latter was a collection of loud, powerful love songs interspersed with more reflective pieces such as 'Downhill from Here', all sung with conviction by Hansard and played with no little skill by the whole band. Island were seemingly dissatisfied with both the material and the progress, however, and The Frames were dropped soon after. It was to be the first of many such reverses.

Disappointed but unbroken, the band decided to plough a more independent furrow with their own DC label. Hansard returned from a trip to the US with the songs that would by and large make up the next album, *Fitzcarraldo* (1995), named after a film directed by Werner Herzog and starring Klaus Kinski. This self-financed product came to the attention of big-shot English producer Trevor Horn, who signed the band to his ZTT label and rereleased the album (and two singles, 'Monument' and 'Revelate') the following year in a slightly different package. The connection with Horn, who had an impressive roster of acts signed to his label, promised much, and again the band and their supporters were hopeful. When the mainstream breakthrough still didn't come, however, ZTT attempted to dictate both musical and marketing lines for The Frames to follow. By 1999, when the more studied *Dance the Devil* album was released, the relationship between band and label had soured irretrievably, and The Frames were desperate to escape from what they had come to regard as a totally invidious association. With the frustration of working for an unsympathetic label dispelled, the band began to record the album that would become *For the Birds* (2001), the most successful record (in both critical and commercial terms) they had released up to that time. Lionized at home, as well as by an elite band of foreign cognoscenti, The Frames' stock continued to rise into the new millennium, leaving Hansard and crew awaiting the accidental airplay or mood swing of some major label's managing director that would launch them on the path to world domination that so many had predicted for them.

'Revelate' was first unleashed upon an unsuspecting public in February 1995, accompanied by a video that has gone down in Irish rock annals as probably the least expensive and most effective ever produced. That aside, few could resist the fierce energy which The Frames managed to instil in this record. It might be a love song (or, more specifically, a 'hate' song); it might be about destructive self-accusation; it might be addressed to the oblivious spirit that orders human experience; it might be all and none of these things, but it hardly matters. The modulation from the C#m of the verse to the E of the chorus, and Hansard's alternation of a quivering 'pop' vocal in the former and full-throated 'rock' voice in the latter, drags the listener from one intense emotional state to another without mercy. Seldom has vulnerability sounded so aggressive, or failure so defiant. Here was an anthem for all those (which includes just about everybody on the planet) who at some point have 'fucked it up' and are in need of redemption. The final moments, in which Hansard cries 'Redeem yourself' three times at the top of his range, are profoundly cathartic ones in which the singer, the 'you' whom he has addressed throughout the song and the listener are drawn together in an identification of the perennial human story that tells of the inevitability of pain and the necessity for release.

Hansard and The Frames continue to inspire deep levels of devotion amongst certain sections of the Irish popular-music-loving public. Others find the intensity too intense and the integrity too … well, too much. It's only rock 'n' roll, after all. Regardless of your position on this, what The Frames do offer is a clear example of a dialectic that emerges occasionally in rock discourse between the music and a peculiar extra-musical aura with which a band or an individual comes to be surrounded. 'Revelate' could only have been performed by The Frames and could only have been sung by Glen Hansard; that a song *belongs* to a singer in such a way, that a singer is *realized* through a song in such a way, presents us with a mystery that goes to the heart of the rock dream.

Best Bit: The beginning and the end. And the middle.

What Can I Do?

THE CORRS [ATLANTIC]

The small town of Dundalk – located eleven miles south of the northern border – became notorious in the late 1990s for harbouring members of the self-proclaimed Real IRA – a vicious Republican splinter group that was responsible for some of the North's most violent episodes, including the appalling bomb attack at Omagh in 1998. The town's new-found reputation for militant nationalism only worsened its existing profile as a dreary provincial settlement that passing tourists recognized as the midway point between Dublin and Belfast.

It was especially ironic, then, that Dundalk should produce Ireland's most glamorous pop outfit, The Corrs. The band came together in 1990 when Jim Corr (keyboards, guitar, vocals) recruited his younger sisters Andrea (vocals, tin whistle), Caroline (drums, bodhran, piano, vocals) and Sharon (violin, vocals) for a family-based pop-rock project. From The Jacksons to The Nolans, via The Carpenters and The Osmonds, there has been a long tradition of bands presenting themselves as families, 'trading' (in the words of Dave Laing) 'on the association between musical and domestic harmony'. Of course, this often belies fractious sibling disharmony, but The Corrs would always maintain a professional veneer of cheery consensus.

Coming from a strong musical family (the band's parents had played in a local lounge act) the young Corrs were exposed to a wide variety of musical styles, from folk and trad to 1970s easy-listening fare like The Eagles, The Carpenters and Fleetwood Mac. Such reference points were clearly audible in the evolving Corrs' sound, with the group incorporating a dash of diddly-eye in their synthesized pop-rock aesthetic.

It was during the filming of *The Commitments* (1991) that the band first came to public attention, with Andrea playing Jimmy Rabbitte's younger sister while her siblings took brief cameo roles. The film's musical director, John Hughes, was so impressed by the youngsters that he volunteered to be their manager, mapping out a 'ten-year plan' for global success. The first few years of the project brought scant reward, with UK and Irish labels showing little interest in the group. In 1994, however, Jean Kennedy Smith – then US Ambassador to Ireland – witnessed a Corrs show at Whelan's Pub in Dublin, and invited them to play at a World Cup event in Boston. The band quickly found themselves in the US, performing acoustic showcase gigs along the East Coast. After one such event in New York, they audaciously blagged their way into the famous Hit

Factory studio, demanding an impromptu audition with Michael Jackson-producer David Foster.

The producer was instantly smitten by the group, and agreed to oversee their debut album, *Forgiven, Not Forgotten* (1995), after getting the band a deal with Atlantic Records. Lead-off single 'Runaway' (1995) made an immediate impression in the US, launching the group's carefully cultivated pop persona, which reconciled the 'lovely girl' image of Dana with a glossy veneer of MTV sensuality. The three sisters quickly became Ireland's first pop starlets (or 'the sex Nolans', as *Sky* magazine put it). Belying their often ethereal appearance, though, was hard graft and genuine talent, with the quartet picking up a reputation as 'the hardest-working band in showbusiness'. Gruelling world tours with the likes of Celine Dion followed, paving the way for follow-up album *Talk on Corners* (1997). Shifting over nine million copies, the album became The Corrs' breakthrough record and most successful effort to date. Co-produced by Glen Ballard – fresh from success with Alanis Morrissette's *Jagged Little Pill* (1995) – the record spawned several hit singles, including 'What Can I Do?'.

Originally stalling at a lowly No. 53 in the UK chart, the single's sedate tenor and gentle fiddle track sat incongruously with the late 1990s penchant for techno and house. Noting the industry's new-found taste for dance-pop aesthetics (this was after all the year of *Spiceworld* and U2's 'Discotheque'), the band teamed up with UK remix outfit Tin

· ·

Best Bit: The first few moments of the second chorus (1.25–1.35), furnishing the track with a sublime pop moment.

· ·

Tin Out. Retaining the song's original arrangement and individual performances, the new version introduced some much-needed sparkle, with a freshly recorded guitar part dominating the mix.

Kicking-off with Jim's heavily chorused Telecaster motif, the guitarist stutters out an A9, before dropping the root note to G# and ascending to D9 and E9). Making a simple blues figure sound deceptively contemporary, the riff is a self-consciously derivative allusion to Edie Brickell and The New Bohemians' 1989 college hit, 'What I Am'. With this – and a mid-paced rhythm track – supplying the song's stripped-down musical setting, Andrea's silky voice is rendered all the more striking. Augmenting her tender delivery with strong melodic lines, the lyric conveys yearning for an apparently taciturn lover ('I haven't slept at all in days / It's been so long since we've talked'). After a similarly sparse chorus section in which the singer's voice steps up a range ('What can I do to make you love me? What can I do to make you care?'), the second verse is underscored by a simple bass line and high-register synth motif. Andrea's vocal is now more assured (displaying an unmistakably American accent), setting up a highly affecting second chorus, in which an elegant string section provides some dramatic 'middle' between the singer's voice and an unusually low synth-bass.

Switching to F#m for a simple middle eight, the singer's descending vocal brings to mind Karen Carpenter ('No more waiting, no more aching ...'). Finally resolving this 'ache' by embracing human fate ('Because the power is not mine / I'm just going to let it fly'), she is joined for a reassuring final chorus by her sisters' multi-layered vocal harmonies. Restoring the track's middle eight for a dramatic coda, the singer offers a rhetorical plea ('love me') to the song's absent lover, evoking the Motown girl groups of the 1960s, whose songs frequently called out to imaginary male characters.

Reaching No. 3 in the UK in 1998, 'What Can I Do?' heightened the group's profile ahead of *In Blue* (1999), which went straight to the top of the charts. Going on to become Europe's bestselling Irish act for the period 1996–2001, the group shifted fourteen million albums in that continent alone. Picking up several Grammy nominations and Brit Awards along the way, The Corrs – like *Riverdance* and *Ballykissangel* – embodied a highly palatable brand of post-Celtic Tiger Irishness. A transnational pop phenomenon from Turin to Tokyo, their inoffensive youthful glamour chimed perfectly with the new image of Irish migrants as aspirant, middle class and professional.

Appearing at the 1998 Commonwealth Games in Kuala Lumpur endeared the group little to Dundalk's hardline nationalists (the Republic had cut ties with Britain's 'family of nations' in 1949), and rock purists continued to wince at their unashamedly commercial brand of saccharine pop. Notwithstanding the band's definitive statement of rock 'authenticity' – an MTV *Unplugged* set in 1999 – they have done themselves few favours, signing sponsorship deals with Lloyds Bank and Pepsi, before joining forces with IMG (the world's leading marketing agency), whose roster includes Tiger Woods, the Williams sisters and Manchester United. An opportunistic attempt to break into the Hispanic market with an Alejandro Sanz collaboration, 'One Night' (2001) – as well as an unfortunate appearance on *Beverley Hills 90210* – scarcely helped matters. In fairness to the group, though, they've taken Irish music to some fairly extraordinary arenas, including the Vatican, the White House and Buckingham Palace. If bringing pop glamour to Dundalk wasn't enough, their performances for two US Presidents, one Pope and a Queen surely deserve recognition. For this alone, we salute them.

National Express

THE DIVINE COMEDY [SETANTA]

Northern Irish rock in the late 1990s was dominated by the sound of hard-edged garage punk, with acts like Therapy? and Ash maintaining the province's reputation for high-octane power-pop. Indeed, Therapy? had produced Ulster's most successful single of all time in 'Screamager' (1993), a Top Five UK hit seen by many as a northern classic to rival 'Teenage Kicks' and 'Alternative Ulster'. It wasn't all blistering punk metal north of the border, however, as witnessed by Belfast 'house' DJ David Holmes, whose breakthrough album, *Let's Get Killed* (1997), spawned two Top Forty hit singles in 'Don't Die Just Yet' (1998) and 'My Mate Paul' (1998).

The North's star act of 1998, however, was a chintzy cabaret-rock outfit called The Divine Comedy. Founder member and front man Neil Hannon – the son of an Anglican clergyman – had been reared in Enniskillen, where he attended the famous Portora Royal School (alma mater of Oscar Wilde and Samuel Beckett). Reacting against the social conservatism of his middle-class background, Hannon formed The Divine Comedy in his late teens, moving to London with a couple of schoolfriends and striking a deal with Irish indie label Setanta. The singer had witnessed REM's legendary show at Dublin's RDS in June 1989, and debut effort *Fanfare for the Comic Muse* (1990) clearly displayed the influence of the Athens quartet. This early incarnation of The Divine Comedy would quickly disband, however, with Hannon retreating to his parents' house for an eighteen-month sabbatical.

Taking on a new set of influences, most notably Noel Coward, Jacques Brel and Scott Walker, this creative hiatus culminated in the release of *Liberation* (1993), critically acclaimed but commercially unsuccessful. The diminutive Hannon was already cultivating his signature dandy persona – replete with tailored suits and dark sunglasses – whilst conjuring artful titles like 'The Pop Singer's Fear of the Pollen Count' (1993). Follow-up *Promenade* (1994) consolidated this effort, paving the way for breakthrough album *Casanova* (1996). Recorded with a new line-up, the album introduced elegant string, brass and orchestral textures to the band's idiosyncratic cabaret-rock aesthetic. Hannon also refined his increasingly comic instincts, penning the theme tune for TV comedy *Father Ted,* a version of which appears on the album as 'Songs of Love'. With the support of a Top Twenty hit single, 'Something for the Weekend', Hannon became a mainstream pop celebrity. Like Pulp's Jarvis Cocker, the singer's foppish appearance and witty song lyrics contravened Britpop's masculine codes, but this did little to hinder

the group's success, with follow-up singles 'Becoming More Like Alfie (1996) and 'The Frog Princess' (1996) both reaching the UK Top Thirty.

After completing *A Short Album About Love* (1997) – a live recording of new material performed with a thirty-piece orchestra – the band began work on their fourth album proper, *Fin de Siècle* (1998). Recorded in two weeks, the album took a more introspective form than its predecessors, with Hannon tapping into pre-millennial angst on tracks like 'Here Comes the Flood'. Described by many critics as a 'concept album', it also included Hannon's first address to the Troubles on 'Sunrise', the album's reflective finale. In the context of 1998's historic peace initiative, the Good Friday Agreement, Hannon offered a tender meditation on the Ulster crisis, oblivious to the fact that *Fin de Siècle* would be issued in the immediate aftermath of Northern Ireland's most violent episode, a Real IRA bomb attack on the small town of Omagh, which claimed the lives of 29 people and injured 300 others. In this sombre context, Hannon's song seemed tragically prescient, giving the record a gravitas that sat incongruously with the singer's reputation as a postmodern light entertainer. Nevertheless, *Fin de Siecle* became the band's most successful album to date, reaching No. 9 in the UK and spawning their first Top Ten single, 'National Express'.

Propelled by a cheery big-band brass figure (evoking the faux-elegant world of *Come Dancing*), the song's jaunty Motown shuffle and jangly guitar motif (Dmaj7–Am7) furnish a neat backcloth for Hannon's louche baritone. The lyrics – an ironic eulogy for the UK's best-known coach company – are marked by the singer's precise phrasing, his Sinatra-like sincerity heightening the tune's comic tension: 'Take the National Express when your life's in a mess / It'll make you smile.' Playing on this incongruity between style and subject, Hannon reimagines the bus as a microcosm of the nation ('All human life is here'). Casting himself as the coolly detached voyeur, the singer nonchalantly unveils unpleasant truths (via subtle invocations of child abuse and suicide) lying beneath the happy façade of this mobile community.

After a collectively sung chorus section conjures the kitsch world of Hollywood show tunes ('And everybody sings "ba ba ba da …"'), Hannon launches into the mischievous second verse, its sneering condescension tempered by an apparently genuine affection for the 'jolly hostess' who sells 'crisps and tea' for 'a sky-high fee'. However, this merely serves as preface to the coarse final couplet: 'Mini-skirts were in style when she danced down the aisle back in '63 / But it's hard to get by when your arse is the size of a small country.'

Hannon's ostensibly ironic delivery invited post-feminist listeners to take this sentiment with a pinch of salt. And though his lyrics had occasionally displayed chauvinistic impulses in the past (not least on the band's previous album, *Casanova*), 'National Express' had an entirely different agenda. Like Portora old boy Oscar Wilde, Hannon was busy cultivating the role of displaced Irish dandy in London, inhabiting that curious insider/outsider position that enabled Wilde to satirize taken-for-granted British institutions with equal measures of affection and contempt. Focusing our attention on the humdrum world of public transport, Hannon offers an ironic commentary on the peculiarities of English life, celebrating the mundane and commonplace whilst satirizing human pretence and insincerity. Thus, in a brief middle-eight break, the singer skilfully parodies cheesy TV transport commercials, his filtered voice evoking the sound of a bus depot announcer ('Don't just sit there feeling stressed / Take a trip on the National Express'). A bluesy guitar solo then prefaces Hannon's whispered mantra of the song's title, replicating the repetitive rhythms of road travel for a full minute and a half, before the track quietly segues into an unrestrained sax and wind exchange.

Consolidating the success of *Fin de Siècle* with an anthology, *A Secret History* (1999), the band signed with major label Parlophone for their next long-player, *Regeneration* (2001). By this stage, Hannon's fanciful fop persona was veering towards self-parody, and he responded by (literally) letting his hair down, trading his signature suits for T-shirt and jeans, and reverting to the band's primary colours (guitar, bass, drums). Overseen

Best Bit: At 2.32, Hannon's mock-sincere middle-eight refrain ('Tomorrow belongs to me'), prompted by the track's brief detour from an otherwise insistent 'home' chord.

by Radiohead producer Nigel Godrich, the album showcased some of Hannon's most melancholic moments, and least accessible material. Unsurprisingly, critical praise was not matched by chart success, and, after a brief Irish tour, Hannon controversially sacked his bandmates before performing solo acoustic dates – as The Divine Comedy – in the US. Whatever the future holds for Hannon, he has left Northern Irish rock with some of its most refined art-pop moments. Old Oscar would've been proud.

October Swimmer

JJ72 [LAKOTA]

The final year of the millennium was a mixed one in Ireland. While millions of people witnessed the summer's historic solar eclipse, few could ignore the fact that Irish rock had itself become obscured by the country's innumerable boy (and girl) bands (Boyzone, Westlife, B*Witched). This strand of highly synthetic bland pop – which made perfect sense amongst post-Britney pre-teens – was partly a symptom of music industry change. Like all mass-producing businesses, popular music has its default position, and with declining sales after the demise of Britpop, the industry turned to its failsafe formula of low-cost teenybop.

In an Irish context, this abrupt pop turn made radio-friendly acts like The Corrs sound like an Authentic Rock Experience. Indeed, the Dundalk multi-instrumentalists went on to become that year's big Irish live draw, with an enormous homecoming show at Dublin's Landsdowne Road. But mid-Atlantic Celt-rock wasn't the country's only riposte to pop svengali Louis Walsh. In fact, there was a growing frustration with pop-Irishry of any hue (be it Westlife or The Corrs), thus Mark Greaney's insistence that his band, JJ72, were in fact a bunch of 'West Brits' for whom 'Irish music meant nothing'. Still a teenager at the end of the 1990s, Greaney would later pen a tune called 'Oíche Mhaith' (Irish for 'good night'), but his muse was always more Camus than Comhaltas, drawing on English miserabilists like Joy Division and Nick Drake rather than homegrown folk, rock or diddly-eye.

The songwriter was still attending Dublin's Belvedere College (Jesuitical alma mater to James Joyce) when he hooked up with classmate (and fellow school 'outsider') Fergal Matthews. Marginalized by the school's macho-sports consensus, they quickly recast themselves as JJ72, taking their enigmatic moniker from a Belvedere window pane made out of 72 jam jars. (Greaney has been famously reticent about revealing this fact in press interviews, fuelling endless speculation about the band's name on numerous fan-based websites). Modelling themselves on classic indie three-pieces like Nirvana and The (post-1996) Manic Street Preachers, Greaney (vocals, guitar) and Matthews (drums) auditioned a series of bass players before settling on Hilary Woods. A classically trained pianist and ballerina, Woods became the latest in rock's illustrious cast of female bass players, following spiritual predecessors like Tina Weymouth (Talking Heads), Kim Gordon (Sonic Youth) and Kim Deal (The Pixies). She would also become a bona fide pop pin-up, with journalists incessantly referencing her 'kohl-rimmed Egyptian eyes', and *Melody Maker* proclaiming her 'the sexiest woman in rock'.

Playing their first date with Woods at Dublin's Trinity College, the group's material was bleak and introspective, with Greaney wearing his angst-rock influences on his sleeve. Consequently, while they quickly established themselves as a highly visceral live act (with a propensity to trash their own equipment), comparisons were frequently made with the band's current heroes (Placebo, The Smashing Pumpkins, Radiohead). What made for a truly distinctive sound, however, was Greaney's unusual vocal, an arresting falsetto squall that led many listeners to assume that he was in fact a girl. Described by *Record Collector* as 'Jeff Buckley skydiving with Brian Molko', his delivery was derided elsewhere as 'an oestrogen-fuelled chipmunk squeak'.

If Greaney's vocal style went against the grain of Britpop's 'laddish' masculinity, the singer also reacted against pop's unashamed anti-intellectualism, cultivating a bookish persona that gave JJ72 a reputation as precocious pop aesthetes. A famous promo shot of the band clutching works of classic literature (they had only recently passed their Leaving Cert exams) unsurprisingly provoked some harsh criticism, with *Hot Press* describing the diminutive Greaney as 'little Lord Baudelaire'.

Notwithstanding such derision, the group had little trouble finding a record deal, being quickly picked up by Lakota, a Dublin-based subsidiary of Sony. A five-track demo CD, 'Pillows', was soon championed by BBC DJ Mark Radcliffe, paving the way for debut single 'October Swimmer' (1999). Fading in with a quiet arpeggio on acoustic guitar, Greaney switches from an unresolved variant of C major to C itself for the song's breathy opening line ('the dreams of dying mothers …'). Using a reassuringly familiar chord sequence (C–Am) – typical of introspective indie-rock ballads like The Smiths' 'I Know It's Over' (1986) and Jeff Buckley's reworking of 'Hallelujah' (1994) – each line modulates toward the inevitable minor key.

Perhaps with Buckley in mind, Greaney kicks off at a fairly high vocal register, climbing even further when Hilary's single-note bass-line marks a simple inter-verse refrain (Dm–G). This ascending vocal/falling bass contrast makes for an interesting set of gender relations within the band, for although Woods was originally chosen for her unambiguously feminine good looks, here she performs a stereotypically 'masculine' function. Furnishing the song with its solid foundation, the bass player's unfussy root notes stand against Greaney's wailing falsetto (connoting a more conventionally 'feminine' sensibility). This is more than a little ironic, not least because the singer was once a neighbour of Ireland's quintessential 'cock rock' bass-player/vocalist, Phil Lynott.

Brightening the tune's hitherto sparse mix with a reverberating Strat and strummed acoustic, Greaney enunciates the song's title for the first and only time ('the splash of October swimmers'). Based on a story told to Greaney by his artist mother (about a man she had seen swimming in freezing conditions), the lyrics are marked by the singer's unrelenting teen-angst, not least during his memorable 'I want to be a happy boy' refrain. Boosted by some fast-paced thrashing guitars and Fergal's staccato snare, the song's anomie may (as Greaney claims) have been informed by a more universal sense of pre-millennial tension. But even if this were the case, his neurotic choirboy vocals inexorably tie 'October Swimmer' to an unambiguously adolescent context. Rather ironically, then, the song – for all its hard-edged indie aesthetics – may have had more in common with Ireland's boy-band pop ballads than Greaney wished to acknowledge.

Released in time for Dublin's staging of the 1999 MTV Europe Awards, 'October Swimmer' benefited from very little media exposure, with Lakota issuing only 500 copies of the original single. Nevertheless, the record did become 'Single of the Week' on Mark Radcliffe's radio show, and the band quickly established themselves as *Top of the Pops* regulars, with a string of follow-up singles – including a re-released 'October Swimmer' (2000) – all making the UK Top Thirty.

This paved the way for the group's eponymous debut album, which went straight into the UK chart at No. 16. Memorable festival appearances followed (including Glastonbury, Reading and Witnness), before the JJ's took a highly prestigious support slot with U2 at Slane Castle. Receiving the 'Best New Band' accolade at the 2001 Irish

Best Bit: Greaney's skilfully controlled feedback during the song's fading coda (3.00–3.18), recalling Neil Young's ground-breaking work on *Arc* (1991).

Music Awards, they quickly began work on follow-up album, *I to Sky* (2002). A more upbeat and less upfront affair than its predecessor, the record displayed an increasing maturity, showcasing live favourites like 'Formulae' and 'Sinking'.

Reaching the Top Twenty in the UK, *I to Sky* promised more than it actually delivered, and news of Hilary's departure in 2003 shocked the group's sizeable fanbase. But with new recruit Sarah Fox taking up Woods's position, the band soon began work on a third album. It remains to be seen if JJ72 can realize Greaney's full potential, but it's worth noting that they have at least outlived most of their Irish pop contemporaries, with Boyzone and B*Witched disbanded, and Westlife falling by the wayside. Pop is dead, long live rock!

2000

Beautiful Day

U2 [ISLAND]

By the turn of the millennium, U2 had become Ireland's best-known export in any field. Two decades earlier, their debut album, *Boy* (1980), had launched a career that would take them from the Dandelion Market to ZOO TV via evangelical Christianity, white flags and Live Aid. Landmark albums like *The Joshua Tree* (1987) and *Achtung Baby* (1991), meanwhile, had ensured the group's iconic status in rock history.

In the late 1990s, though, U2 were in the unusual position of having to dream up a successful 'comeback' record after the critical and commercial shortcomings of *Pop* (1997). This album had been bravely conceived as a techno-rock experiment, but came to a hasty conclusion when the band – who had committed themselves to a world tour before completing the record – ran out of time. The album itself received poor notices, but when an obviously under-rehearsed U2 hit the live stage (via a 40-foot lemon), the knives really came out. 'If hubris has a sound,' claimed the UK's *Observer* newspaper, 'then this is it.' As Larry Mullen, U2's drummer, will tell you, few bands would be expected to recover from such grand-scale humiliation. Yet, under extraordinary pressure (not to mention significant public disinterest), U2 returned with one of the best sets of their career, *All That You Can't Leave Behind* (2000), followed by an outstanding sell-out tour. What's the story of this enduring outfit? And how have they maintained their position as Ireland's premier rock act?

The band famously came together at the progressive, multi-denominational Mount Temple School in Dublin's northside in the late 1970s. Their attendance at this unique institution was indicative of the group's diverse family backgrounds. For although U2's founding member, Larry Mullen, had a conventional Irish Catholic upbringing, his musical cohorts were marginalized from Catholic Ireland in a variety of ways. Bono, the group's vocalist and lyricist, came from a 'mixed' background, and was initially raised in the (Protestant) Church of Ireland. Guitarist The Edge, meanwhile,

was born in London to a Welsh Presbyterian family, while Adam Clayton, the group's Oxfordshire-born bass player, had an English Protestant upbringing.

Feeling a sense of dislocation from 'straight' society (Bono claims he 'didn't know whether [he] was working class, middle class, Protestant, Catholic, English, American or Irish'), the group formed a symbolic community of their own, 'Lypton Village'. A loose coalition of friends and musicians, Village life offered a surrealistic riposte to the rigidly masculine 'bootboy' culture of late 1970s Dublin, spawning two very different – though closely related – rock bands, The Virgin Prunes and The Hype. The latter were an unexceptional post-punk outfit; they later became U2.

After a couple of moderately successful Irish-only singles, 'U2-3' (1979) and 'Another Day' (1980), the band underwent a remarkable metamorphosis. Edge picked up a Memory Man Echo Unit, enabling him to develop his signature style of high-register riffs and resounding harmonics. Underpinned by Adam's pumping bass and Larry's solid snare, the band's increasingly expansive sound took shape around Bono's anthemic vocals, audibly foregrounded in the reverberation of early efforts *Boy* (1980), *October* (1981) and *War* (1983).

Feeling that they had painted themselves into a corner, the band began to experiment with more abstract terrain on the Brian Eno-produced *Unforgettable Fire* (1984), its highly atmospheric textures anticipating the widescreen ambience of *The Joshua Tree* (1987), which fused the direct, emotional appeal of U2's live shows with an increasingly refined approach to songwriting and production. By this stage, U2 had become the biggest rock band on the planet, and ridiculous over-exposure – via the *Rattle and Hum* album, book and movie (1988) – was starting to tarnish a hard-won reputation. Thus, at the turn of the new decade, an emotionally drained Bono would publicly concede – in the face of relentless press criticism – that U2 would have to 'go away, and dream it all up again'.

Achtung Baby (1991) famously signalled the birth of U2 Mark II, introducing fresh sensibilities (playfulness, sexuality, darkness, doubt) to the band's mosaic, and sparking a long-term fascination with various kinds of dance and industrial music. This experiment continued – with varying degrees of success – on *Zooropa* (1993), *Original Soundtracks 1* (1995) and *Pop* (1997), before the band returned to more familiar terrain on *All That You Can't Leave Behind* (2000).

Effortlessly combining the idealism, sincerity and expansive textures of U2 Mark I (1980–88) with the irony, restraint and experimentation of their second phase (1991–7), the album is a perfect synthesis of the U2 aesthetic. Eno and Daniel Lanois expertly revitalize the band's most compelling soundscapes, while Bono's freshly clipped vocals are neatly complemented by Edge's new-found enthusiasm for the guitar. Showcasing some of the best material of their career ('In A Little While', 'Kite', 'New York'), the album paints a picture of a band that has wrestled with its own contradictions and now feels at ease with itself, happy to trade the earnestness of innocence for the ache of experience. 'I'm not afraid of anything in this world / There's nothing you can throw at me that I haven't already heard,' as Bono announces in the opening line of 'Stuck in a Moment You Can't Get Out Of'.

Opening track and lead-off single 'Beautiful Day' is perhaps the most striking instance of this sensibility. Prefaced by Eno's ethereal synth-loop, a pulsating bass drum foreshadows one of Bono's most arresting opening lines ('The heart is a bloom, shoots up through the stony ground'). Opting for an unusually intimate spoken-sung

Best Bit: The song's final section (3.14–3.46) in which Bono's impassioned vocal combines with Edge's signature guitar tones to conjure up a sound that hadn't been heard since the halcyon days of the *Boy* tour.

delivery, the vocalist rekindles the warmth of early U2 in a knowingly upbeat – rather than earnestly naive – manner. Meanwhile, Adam's signature bass line sets up the song's central chord cycle (A–Bm–D–G–D–A), before Edge plugs in his trusty old Gibson Explorer and Memory Man Echo Unit. The guitar player's serene brush strokes teasingly evoke the 'classic' U2 aesthetic of *The Joshua Tree*, while Eno's intermittent synth-tones – and a heavily reverberated Edge/Lanois backing vocal – fill in the gaps. None of this prepares the listener, however, for the visceral double-speed chorus, its distorted barre chords recapturing U2's early apprenticeship as a Ramones cover band.

'Beautiful Day' was more than an exercise in U2 'retro', though, for the song sounded remarkably fresh, even making a nod to contemporary electronica, not least during the spiralling keyboard motif in the slow-paced middle eight. At times, Bono is craftily self-reflexive, undercutting his own sentiment with a rhythmically awkward couplet ('You love this town / Even if that doesn't ring true'), but his unrestrained 'Touch me' refrain – in tandem with Edge's chiming guitar riff – is about as heartfelt as rock music gets.

Many critics picked up on the song's apparent dig at Celtic Tiger Dublin ('There's no room, no space to rent in this town'). However, the track – though inspired by a real-life millionaire who abandoned his riches – had a more universal resonance. More than anything else, it was about a band striving to reconcile its contradictory impulses, joyously celebrating where it was at, whilst finally coming to terms with where it was from. All that you can't leave behind, indeed.

Burn Baby Burn

ASH [INFECTIOUS]

If there's one defining characteristic of the bands from Ulster that we've looked at throughout this book it would have to be: energy. From the raw rhythm 'n' blues of Them, through the pop- and agit-punk of The Undertones and Stiff Little Fingers, to the proto-nu-metal of Therapy?, Northern Irish rockers aren't afraid to rip it up big time. Allied to this is the propensity of such bands to utilize the '11' setting on their amps. Socio-political speculation as to the preponderance of loud, fast guitar bands from the North belongs elsewhere; here, it's enough to note the tradition and to accept the influence it will inevitably have on successive generations of young musicians.

The tradition of noisy, energetic, guitar-driven pop is one in which we may locate Ash. Guitarist/vocalist Tim Wheeler, bassist Mark Hamilton and drummer Rick 'Rock' McMurray were famously still at school in the small County Down town of Downpatrick when they began to make an impression on the UK charts in the mid-1990s. Championed from an early stage by *New Musical Express,* Ash played pop-punk anthems about (in no particular order) *Star Wars,* kung fu, girls and summer, and the indie-loving public lapped it up. A string of brilliant singles throughout 1995 and 1996 presaged the release of the band's first proper album, *1977* (1996), which went to the top of the UK charts amid rave reviews, making Ash the first Irish band to reach the UK No. 1 with their debut album. Subsequent events showed that the three young Ulstermen were prepared to walk the walk as well as talk the talk. With English guitarist Charlotte Hatherley added to the line-up, the band continued to play hard and party harder over the following years, taking in peace concerts, commissions (for the film *A Life Less Ordinary*) and boy-band-baiting along the way.

The golden summer seemed to have ended, however, with the approach of their twenties and the release of a second album, *Nu-Clear Sounds* (1998), a record which only made No. 15 in the charts and which most critics found less satisfying than their debut. There followed a fallow year when Wheeler returned to his parents' home in Downpatrick to recover from burn-out, and to write the material which would comprise the band's third major studio album, *Free All Angels* (2001).

The same critics who had predicted the bursting of the bubble after *Nu-Clear Sounds* were ecstatic over the new record, a No. 1 which went on to win all sorts of awards and catapulted Ash to the A-list of contemporary rock bands. Recorded in the south of Spain over a two-month period, *Free All Angels* saw Wheeler and Co. determined to produce an all-killer, no-filler album, chock-full of potential singles, with nothing that would make anyone want to reach for the CD remote. They had about thirty original Wheeler compositions from which to choose, and on its release it was clear that the main man's time back in the old town hadn't been wasted.

Almost immediately, people began to make comparisons with The Beach Boys. *1977* was Ash's *Surfin' Safari* (1962), a brilliant opening statement which significantly extended the horizons of what was currently available in the pop world. Just as *Beach Boys' Party!* (1966) reflected the Californian group's uncertainty as to their direction after a long period churning out minor variations upon that original statement, so *Nu-Clear Sounds* saw Ash hesitating about what they and others expected of the band. Which brings us, of course, to one of contemporary pop music's defining moments, the masterpiece that was and is *Pet Sounds* (1966) – a record with no filler, twelve potential hits, and an overarching theme in terms of lyrics and sound. Brian Wilson's achievement on *Pet Sounds* was to successfully combine his evolving technological mastery with a traditional, yet absolutely contemporary, pop sensibility. Which is to say: Wilson distilled the established pop themes of joy and sorrow, fear and desire, that had gone into earlier

· ·

Best Bit: The layered intro in which speaker-hopping feedback is followed by lead-guitar figure, bass, snare roll and rhythm guitar, until they all come together, just the way the goddess intended.

· ·

Beach Boys recordings, and then brought a uniquely imaginative studio technique to bear upon them, making an album that had wide mainstream appeal yet was deeply personal, that was timeless in many respects, yet completely of its moment.

Large boots to fill, indeed, and despite his admiration for the great man, Wheeler had no such pretensions (although he did sample some of *Pet Sounds* for an abortive version of one of the tracks on *Free All Angels,* 'Pacific Palisades'). But the similarities remain striking. Besides the obvious thematic parallels – young love, sex, the joys and the blues of summertime, and so on – there's the fact that both men were twenty-three, both fully tapped into the prevailing popular musical codes of their eras, and both writing 'pop' songs that *sound* familiar yet have unsettling lyrical and musical elements. You could say that Wilson was too old to be composing teenage pop songs such as 'Wouldn't It Be Nice', just as Wheeler was probably too old to be writing about 'walkin' barefoot all summer'. But the thing about the material on *Free All Angels,* as on *Pet Sounds,* is that there's no irony, no descent into cynicism. The teenage emotions are refined rather than rejected or mocked, the 'love' that animated the sixteen-year-old is acknowledged as a purer form of the 'love' sought by the twenty-three-year-old, or, for that matter, the forty- or sixty-three-year-old. *Free All Angels* is not a retread of *1977* after the sophomore angst of *Nu-Clear Sounds,* but an amalgam of both, as well as a reconfirmation of the band's commitment to the goddess of punk-pop.

On an album of memorable tracks, 'Burn Baby Burn' is the first among equals. Like 'Wouldn't It Be Nice', it's a song about teenage sex, or rather, the lack of it. Whereas Wilson's protagonists look forward to the day when they'll be able to consummate their passion, Wheeler's couple are in the throes of a break-up. Everyone knows what Them's Gloria would have done presented with the possibility, so why, he wonders, is she holding out on him? The 'feelings that [he] can't disguise' cannot be reconciled with the alternative moral code that's preventing her from taking it beyond, rather than 'almost to', the point of no return. Mutual disappointment leads to 'vicious bitter words becoming more and more cruel', and a feeling that 'something inside has died'. So disillusioned is he, indeed, that he doesn't know if it's worth the effort to go through the undeniable sweetness of reconciliation yet again. The music, energized by sexual tension but a bit ungrounded, reflects this uncertainty, modulating during the verses from B to C#, and from E to Em, and then during the chorus from E to A.

Loud guitar pop about sexual frustration shouldn't be this interesting, perhaps, but it's only as interesting as the emotions themselves which, in case you've forgotten, are some of the most fundamental and formative that humans can experience.

Let a Good Thing Go

GEMMA HAYES [SOURCE]

The small Tipperary village of Ballyporeen will forever be associated with Ronald Reagan's visit to Ireland in 1984. The US President had traced his family roots back to the village, where he was welcomed by a troupe of traditional Irish set-dancers. Amongst the dancers was one Gemma Hayes, a local six-year-old who would go on to make a living out of live performance, albeit one inspired by a very different kind of American icon: Kurt Cobain.

Like many of her generation, Hayes's epiphanic pop moment came in 1991, when Cobain's band Nirvana released their seminal 'Smells Like Teen Spirit' single. Music had always been an important part of the singer's life, with her Garda father (a keyboard player in local duo The Hillbillies) ensuring there were plenty of instruments around the house, and seven older siblings supplying an eclectic soundtrack to Gemma's early years. Consequently, the singer had little difficulty in cultivating wildly divergent tastes, most notably in grungy US rock (Pearl Jam, Nirvana) and mellow British folk (John Martyn, Nick Drake).

It was the latter end of Hayes's taste spectrum that informed her early shows at Dublin's International Bar. By this stage (the late 1990s) the singer had enrolled on an Arts Degree course at University College Dublin, but an increasing commitment to songwriting meant that she had to drop out. Quickly establishing herself on the city's singer-songwriter circuit, Hayes began to feel constrained by her exclusively acoustic repertoire. Switching to a full band set-up, she introduced squalling rock guitars to her sonic palette (owing more to My Bloody Valentine than Suzanne Vega), resulting in her now trademark juxtaposition of delicate country folk and frenetic guitar grunge.

This unusual combination of starkly different styles made Hayes difficult to categorize, with confused music journalists throwing-up terms like 'nu-folk' and 'alt-country', whilst comparing her with Alanis Morrissette, P J Harvey and (bizarrely) Kylie Minogue. To confuse matters further, Hayes had signed with ultra-trendy dance label

Source (home to the likes of Air and Daft Punk), its French techno credentials sitting incongruously with Hayes's rockier Stateside influences.

With a brace of EPs – *4.35 AM* (2001) and *Work to a Calm* (2001) – under her belt, Hayes began sessions for a debut album in upstate New York, with US producer Dave Fridman (of Flaming Lips and Mercury Rev fame) at the helm. Picking up an audibly American singing accent, the waif-like vocalist began to cultivate an East Coast 'college girl' look, with flimsy vests, worn-out jeans and Converse All-Stars (to boot). On stage, she was a model of cool serenity, starkly contrasting with Ireland's better-known female rock figures (Dolores, Sinéad). While serious 'musos' were impressed by Hayes's penchant for classic rock guitars (most notably a vintage Telecaster and Jazzmaster), less erudite fans were drawn by her striking good looks (with the singer attracting the attention of various men's magazines).

With so many paradoxes at work, it was perhaps inevitable that *Night on My Side* (2002) became such a schizophrenic affair, mixing hushed folk fragility with noisy guitar aggression. As if to underline this point, the US edition was reshuffled into (acoustic) 'Night' and (electric) 'Day' sides (with the original title track being left off altogether). In truth, however, the material was held together by Hayes's persistent melancholy, bestowing the set with a narrowly introspective emotional range.

Occasionally veering into Sarah McLachlan (and even Norah Jones) territory, many tracks – such as the remarkable 'Ran for Miles' – wound up on 'Acoustic Chill Out' albums (making *Night on My Side* likely soundtrack material for an episode of *Dawson's Creek*). Elsewhere, however, the set recalls classic US alt-rockers like The Breeders and The Pixies (whom Hayes occasionally covered in concert). Significantly, the grungiest number on the record, 'Let a Good Thing Go', also conjured The Frames, Ireland's most Pixies-fixated band. This was no coincidence, considering the input (including guitar, production and engineering duties) of ex-Frames man Dave Odlum.

Launched by a startlingly muscular guitar figure, the song's heavily layered bursts of discordant white noise are fractured only by Odlum's piercing lead notes (C#–D–A–F#) and a deceptively simple chord change (G–F#m). Abruptly segueing into the sedate first verse, Hayes's carefully measured vocals offer a serene riposte to the band's unrestrained intro. Accompanied by a thick pulsating bass and mid-paced snare, the singer is characteristically introspective ('In the shade of every moment I bled'). Meanwhile, a gently strummed acoustic and quietly shimmering feedback add some colour to the song's shadowy tones, before the jagged intro is unexpectedly restored for a short chorus. Here, the singer offers a cold recital of the song's title ('I let a good thing go'), as if performing some kind of lament.

The track's centrepiece, however, is its double-length second verse, in which Phil Broikos's quietly mixed spoken-sung backing vocals provide Hayes with a subtle (but striking) counter-harmony. Dealing with the melancholic ache of emotional upheaval, this peculiar duet finds the song's narrator in vulnerable mood ('Now every feeling, it kicks me to the bone'). However, there is an increasingly ambivalent acceptance of the song's implied 'loss', with Hayes sounding suspiciously happy during one particular line ('There goes my quiet life I used to keep me warm'). Indeed, by the end of this central stanza, the song's opening couplet has been subtly transformed ('In the shade of this moment I am born'), suggesting an inevitable embrace of emotional growth/ sexual maturity.

With its 'difficult' subject matter and downbeat tenor, 'Let a Good Thing Go' necessarily offers some relief during a brief 'solo' section. However, this proves to be little more than a series of stuttering snares and blunt guitar strikes, with the band quickly making their way back to the song's opening verse. By this stage, Odlum's feedback has become spectacularly eerie, but any uneasiness is ultimately alleviated during the track's upbeat coda, in which a noisily ascending guitar figure offers harmonic closure.

Best Bit: The punctuating drum link (1.16) in the extended second verse ('There goes my quiet life I used to keep me warm').

Fading out with some neatly executed slide guitar, 'Let a Good Thing Go' had 'college-radio hit' written all over it. However, the record had little mainstream impact in the UK or US, despite the fact that *Night on My Side* had received a nomination for the UK's prestigious Mercury Music Prize. Pipped at the post by English rapper Miss Dynamite, Hayes received some consolation when she was voted 'Best Female Singer' by the readers of *Hot Press.*

Perched on the verge of a major breakthrough, the singer became distracted by a long-standing quarrel with Source over record company plans to promote her as a 'sex symbol'. But with these *contretemps* largely resolved, Hayes began sessions for a new album in 2003, returning to Ireland for a high-profile slot at that year's Witness Festival. Playing an extremely well-received set (that included a cover of The Pixies' 'Gigantic'), the *Irish Star* proclaimed Hayes to be the 'Queen of Witness'. It may not be everything, but as British music journalists insist on reminding her, it's a long, long way from Tipperary …

Big Sur

THE THRILLS [VIRGIN]

On I June 2003, the UK's *Observer* newspaper announced the demise of Irish rock music, alerting readers to the apparent dearth of young Irish acts. Admittedly, the London Fleadh had just been cancelled for the first time in its thirteen-year history, but rumours of a 'musical drought' were greatly exaggerated. Notwithstanding the success of singer-songwriters David Kitt and Damien Rice, there was also an emerging avant-garde scene, featuring 'bands' like The Jimmy Cake and The Redneck Manifesto. More importantly, there was Dublin's Thrills, whose 'Big Sur' single (2003) became the year's ubiquitous summer soundtrack.

Though still in their early twenties, the band had been together since the mid-1990s, when childhood pals (and next-door neighbours) Conor Deasy (vocals) and Danny Ryan (guitar) drafted in an old schoolmate Kevin Horan (piano) to form The Cheating Housewives. Ben Carrigan (drums) and Pádraic McMahon (bass) completed the line-up, before the band fashioned a new tag, amalgamating the title of Michael Jackson's best-known album with a Phil Spectorish girl-group moniker.

Though initially seeming like the latest in a long line of post-millennium 'The' bands (The Vines, The Hives, The Strokes, etc.), the sound of The Thrills – variously described as 'blissed-out sunshine pop' and 'scenic landscape indie' – offered a healthy antidote to the ubiquitous garage-punk scene, instigated in the late 1990s by acts like The White Stripes.

Feeling the gravitational pull of America at the end of the 1990s, the young Dubliners decided to follow their muse to California. Exchanging the grey skies of their home town for a long summer in sunny San Diego, the band set up home in a beach hut and began working on a new batch of material. Unsurprisingly, the group's reference points became increasingly West Coast, displaying an especially obvious debt to The Beach Boys, Burt Bacharach, The Byrds and Neil Young. Leavened with a refreshingly contemporary nod to New York rockers The Strokes, The Thrills soon attracted the attention of local Dublin label Supremo, with whom they briefly signed in 2001. Though they left Supremo without releasing a note, the lads were given something of a boost when legendary singer Morrissey dropped by one of their Dublin rehearsal sessions.

Shortly thereafter the band were offered a high-profile support slot at Morrissey's Royal Albert Hall shows, making their UK debut at the prestigious London venue in September 2002. On stage, The Thrills had a peculiar presence, with Deasy hiding his sunburnt good looks behind a tightly gripped mike-stand and Ryan wielding a vintage Telecaster at an unfashionably high chest level (recalling the beat groups of the early 1960s). Nevertheless, the band became a major live draw on the 2003 festival circuit (Glastonbury, Reading, Witness), even securing an esteemed support slot with The Rolling Stones.

Best Bit: The final – and most affecting – chorus section (2.30–3.00), in which the song's Californian setting is memorably conjured by *Pet Sounds*-style backing vocals.

Further celebrity endorsements (Bono, Noel Gallagher) quickly followed, sparking much media attention. In interviews, Deasy and Ryan were articulate and softly spoken (displaying the benefits of a middle-class upbringing in suburban Blackrock), charming a number of major labels before they plumped for Virgin.

A debut EP, 'Santa Cruz', appeared in November 2002, by which time The Thrills were back in California, recording a long-player at LA's Sound Factory with Tony Hoffer (Beck, Supergrass) at the helm. Sartorially, the group cultivated a Californian thrift-store aesthetic, wearing their recycled West Coast influences on their sleeves. Indeed, *So Much for the City* (2003), the band's debut album, often seemed informed by Oscar Wilde's famous maxim 'talent borrows, but genius steals', paying homage to its heroes in a transparently derivative manner. Thus, 'Big Sur' cheekily lifts a lyric from The Monkees theme tune, while 'Your Love Is Like Las Vegas' bears an uncanny resemblance to Bacharach and David's 'Twenty-Four Hours from Tulsa' (1963).

Despite its occasionally ramshackle moments, the album – which entered the UK chart at No. 3 – made for enjoyable listening, offering warm, carefully layered harmonies with an overarching pastoral quality (explicitly conjured by the record's title). At times, its neo-country sensibilities recalled Dublin's late 1980s raggle-taggle scene. (There's also more than a passing resemblance to The Stars of Heaven, one of the great lost voices of Irish rock.) But the band seemed much more interested in escaping – rather than eulogizing – their home town. Thus, they travelled 5,000 miles only to write a song called 'One Horse Town' — an unambiguous repudiation of small-town life ('Does nothing for your state of mind') – that would not sit well on a Saw Doctors album. Released as a single in March 2003, 'One Horse Town' quickly found itself in the UK Top Twenty, paving the way for their next effort, 'Big Sur', in May of that year.

A classic 3-minute pop song, 'Big Sur' starts – somewhat unexpectedly – with the high artifice of Horan's surging synth shapes, before Ryan's impressive banjo-picking establishes the track's unmistakable folk-rock sensibility. An upbeat rhythm section initiates Deasy's delightful opening line – a tender evocation of the album's title – before the singer momentarily unveils a soft Dublin accent ('Tell me that you'll dance to the end / Just tell me that you'll dance to the end').

Once they've established the track's central figure (F–Am–D–F–Am), the band switch to a brief but wistful refrain – in which a falsetto backing vocal emulates the banjo's simple melody – that punctuates each verse. Lyrically, Deasy moves seamlessly from postmodern cheek ('Hey, hey you're the monkees / People said you monkeyed around') to heartrending tenderness ('But nobody's listening now …'). Such gently plaintive tones are thrown into relief, however, when the band hits upon a more upbeat figure (C–F–Dm–G–Em–F) for the classic 'big' chorus. 'Just don't go back to Big Sur', pleads the singer, invoking a whole catalogue of folk and country tunes, not least REM's 'Rockville' (1984).

Admittedly, this section isn't exactly short of ache and yearning, but it also exudes enormous warmth, thanks largely to the music's increasingly layered harmonies. It's Horan's keyboards, though, that provide the subtle backcloth for each successive chorus, furnishing 'Big Sur' with a neat – and reassuringly 'retro' – coda that draws out the song's 'home' chord on a vintage Hammond.

Elsewhere, there are occasional nods to The Byrds, not least in Ryan's brief (and, let it be said, somewhat pedestrian) guitar break, scaling a twelve-string acoustic in the manner of Roger McGuinn. Such allusions are not reserved exclusively for West Coast pop, though, for 'Big Sur' also resonates – albeit in a less obvious manner – with a number of canonical Irish rock tunes. Thus, Deasy's reference to 'letting the old man down' vaguely recalls the similar father-son dynamic in Thin Lizzy's 'Dancing in the Moonlight' (1977), while the song's final line ('Baby, baby please don't go') explicitly evokes classic Them.

Despite such obviously 'retro' sensibilities, The Thrills are very much of their time, typifying the sensibilities of post-Celtic Tiger suburban youth: chilled-out, content and relatively untroubled by Ireland's recent past. And rather ironically, for all its emphasis on flight, excursion and escape, *So Much for the City* often feels quite constrained, its tight, repetitive focus – and occasionally overdone Americana – suggesting that the band will have to undertake a different kind of journey in the future. For all their limitations, though, The Thrills made one thing absolutely certain in 2003: rock 'n' roll Ireland was far from dead and gone.

2004

Chocolate

SNOW PATROL [FICTION]

Ireland's legendary reputation for hospitality and conviviality took something of a knock in 2004, with smokers in the Republic being denied the right to inhale in the country's pubs and clubs, and visiting refugees and asylum-seekers facing stringent new changes to the Republic's Citizenship Law. Meanwhile, US President George W. Bush received a distinctly cold shoulder during his summer stopover at Shannon, where some 8,000 protestors cooked up a notably hostile reception. This may have had something to do with the President's recent instigation of an illegal war, but it was in marked contrast to the mostly warm welcome that Bill Clinton had received only a few years earlier.

On the local music scene, meanwhile, 2004 became the year of the big 'comeback' album, with major new releases from the likes of Ash, The Corrs, The Divine Comedy and U2 (who managed to 'mislay' their new record during a group photo shoot in the south of France). Even The Virgin Prunes – who had broken-up in the mid-1980s – launched a major reissue project, with the band's entire back catalogue being released on CD for the first time. However, there were also some interesting newcomers, not least the quirky Corkonian Simple Kid, whose *SK1* album was nominated for a US Shortlist Prize. Elsewhere, the likes of Damien Rice, Bell Xl and The Future Kings of Spain attracted considerable amounts of critical acclaim. The most celebrated young Irish act of the year, however, was undoubtedly Snow Patrol, whose reissued 2003 album, *Final Straw,* became a massive UK hit, earning the group prestigious Mercury Music Prize and US Shortlist Prize nominations.

The band originally hailed from Belfast but chose to base themselves in the musically vibrant city of Glasgow. Founder members Gary Lightbody (vocals, guitar) and Mark McClelland (bass, keyboards) had met at university in Dundee, before Lightbody's old Belfast schoolmate Jonny Quinn was drafted in on drums. After an initial period as Polar Bear, the band switched to the equally wintry moniker

of Snow Patrol, cultivating a North American alt-rock aesthetic based on The Pixies, Dinosaur Jr and Mercury Rev. More 'brittle pop' than 'Britpop', as one journalist famously put it, The Patrols' distinctively noisy brand of melodic punk pop made for a memorable live experience. However, their first brace of long-players, *Songs for Polar Bears* (1998) and *When It's All Over We Still Have to Clear Up* (2001), failed to translate critical acclaim into commercial sales.

Best Bit: The harmonic relief of the first chorus (1.02–1.08), in which Lightbody invokes the album's title in a rhythmically awkward couplet: 'This is the straw, final straw in the / Roof of my mouth as I lie to you.'

Feeling that their Scottish indie label Jeepster (home of Belle and Sebastian *et al*) couldn't provide them with the support they required, Snow Patrol chose to relocate to Polydor imprint Fiction for their third collection, *Final Straw* (2003–4). With techno producer Garret 'Jacknife' Lee at the helm, and new recruit Nathan Connolly adding extra guitar beef, the band concocted a highly infectious and remarkably accessible new sound that would quickly rescue them from the dreaded 'indie' ghetto. Lightbody's vocals were still breathy and restrained (leading to the inevitable Coldplay comparisons), but the album was a much less fey effort than previous Snow Patrol collections, displaying a new-found fascination for the spiky guitar aesthetics that have characterized so much Ulster rock.

Lacking a strong visual image (an increasingly obligatory requirement in the postmodern video age), the band nevertheless secured a remarkable degree of commercial success, with BBC Radio play-listing key tracks like 'Spitting Games' and 'Run' (which eventually broke the UK Top Ten). Follow-up single 'Chocolate' – issued in time for the group's summer festival performances at the Isle of Wight, Fuji and Glastonbury – deftly weaves together the classic threads of 1980s guitar rock in a fresh and compelling way. Thus, Quinn's staccato drum motif evokes the dramatic intro of The Stone Roses' Madchester anthem, 'I Am the Resurrection' (1989), while McClelland's simple bass figure (D–G) is more than a little reminiscent of *Joshua Tree*-era Adam Clayton. Elsewhere, Connolly's gentle guitar arpeggio conjures the jangling congeniality of Johnny Marr's early Smiths experiments.

With its relentless pounding beat and unashamedly simple structure, 'Chocolate' certainly flirts with monotony. However, Lightbody's heartfelt vocal manages to compel the most unsympathetic listener, while Connolly's vivacious guitar/glockenspiel hook supplies some much needed sparkle and verve. Belying the song's upbeat tempo and the singer's life-affirming opening line ('This could be the very minute / I'm aware I'm alive') is the relatively difficult theme of sexual infidelity ('a simple mistake' that 'starts the hardest time'). What the song offers in this context, however, is a remarkably tender evocation of remorse, with Lightbody's vocal connoting only forgiveness and reconciliation.

These are eminently admirable values of course, particularly in the context of a continuing peace process in Northern Ireland. Indeed, it seems remarkably fitting that this survey of Irish rock should reach its conclusion in Belfast, where our story began forty years ago with Van and Them. (Interestingly, the stomping rhythm and repetitive structure of 'Chocolate' is not dissimilar to 'Gloria'). If nothing else, this underlines the crucial role that Ulster musicians have played in Irish rock culture. As to the future of the island's pop life, we can only guess that various sorts of 'outsider' will continue to lead and innovate in the field. For throughout the form's history, one point has remained resolutely clear: its most influential figures have all been marginalized from mainstream society in various ways. Van, for example, was raised by a Scottish father and Southern Irish mother in a Jehovah's Witness family in East Belfast, while Philo, still the country's most famous black son, was actually born in England to an Irish mother and a Brazilian father. Likewise, Geldof's ancestry lies with Belgian immigrants to Dún Laoghaire, while Bono's background is in a religiously mixed household in the north Dublin hinterland of Ballymun.

Ireland's former Minister for Arts, Culture and the Gaeltacht, Michael D. Higgins, appeared to be on to this point in his 'Economy of the Arts' address in the mid-1990s, when he opined that 'it is in the interstices between cultures that some of the most exciting things happen'. Such 'interstices' – a fertile cultural space that stimulates innovation and new ideas – currently reside in the diverse cultural mix and hybrid identity-fusion of contemporary Ireland, its increasingly multi-ethnic make-up offering a potentially rich resource for the country's future rock culture. If the island is to continue to play a vibrant role at the hub of twenty-first-century popular music, it would do well to recognize that today's immigrants and asylum-seekers may well produce tomorrow's icons and innovators. *Vive le différence! Vive le rock!*

iTunes Playlist

For further information on the songs discussed in this book go to:
http://beautifuldayrock.com

To download a song scroll to the iTunes link and click on: Beautiful Day iMix

Further Reading

Jacques Attali, *Noise: The Political Economy of Music* (1977), trans. Brian Massumi (Manchester: Manchester University Press, 1985)

Stuart Bailie, 'Black Velvet: Ireland's Finest Vinyl', *New Musical Express* (2 June 1990), pp. 18–19

H. Stith Bennett, *On Becoming a Rock Musician* (Amherst: University of Massachusetts Press, 1980)

Tony Bennett *et al* (eds.) *Rock and Popular Music: Politics, Policies, Institutions* (London: Routledge, 1993)

Paul Bew and Henry Patterson, *Seán Lemass and the Making of Modern Ireland, 1945–1966* (Dublin: Gill and Macmillan, 1982)

Andrew Blake (ed.), *Living Through Pop* (London: Routledge, 1999)

Terence Brown, *Ireland: A Social and Cultural History 1922–1985* (London: Fontana, 1985)

Sean Campbell, '"What's the story?": Rock Biography, Musical "Routes" and the Second-Generation Irish in England', *Irish Studies Review*, 12:1 (2004), pp. 63–75

Ciaran Carson, *Last Night's Fun: A Book About Music, Food and Time* (London: Pimlico, 1996)

Peter G. Christenson and Donald F. Roberts, *It's Not Only Rock & Roll: Popular Music in the Lives of Adolescents* (New Jersey: Hampton Press, 1998)

Mary Ann Clawson, 'When women play the bass: Instrument specialization and gender interpretation in alternative rock music', *Gender and Society* 13:2 (1998) pp. 193–210

Tony Clayton-Lea and Rogan Taylor, *Irish Rock: Where It's Come From, Where It's At, Where It's Going* (Dublin: Gill and Macmillan, 1992)

Martin Cloonan, 'Pop and the Nation-State: Towards a Theorisation', *Popular Music* 18:2 (1999), pp. 193–207

Stuart Cosgrove and Sean O'Hagan, 'Gael Force: Two Nations under a Groove – an A to Z of Partisan Pop', *New Musical Express* (2 May 1987), pp. 26–31.

Mark Cunningham, *Good Vibrations: A History of Record Production* (Chessington, Surrey: Sanctuary, 1996)

Robin Denselow, *When the Music's Over: The Story of Political Pop* (London: Faber and Faber, 1989)

Brian Eno, *A Year with Swollen Appendices* (London: Faber and Faber, 1996)

Antony Farrell, Vivienne Guinness and Julian Lloyd (eds.), *My Generation: Rock 'n' Roll Remembered – An Imperfect History* (Dublin: The Lilliput Press, 1996)

Bill Flanagan, *U2 at the End of the World* (London: Bantam Press, 1995)

FORTE Task Force, *Access all Areas: Irish Music – An International Industry. Report to the Minister for Arts, Culture and the Gaeltacht* (Dublin: The Stationery Office, 1996)

Simon Frith, *Sound Effects: Youth, Leisure, and the Politics of Rock 'n' Roll* (New York: Pantheon Books, 1981)

Simon Frith, 'Music and Identity', in Stuart Hall and Paul du Gay (eds.), *Questions of Cultural Identity* (London: Sage, 1996), pp. 108–27

Simon Frith and Andrew Goodwin (eds.) *On Record: Rock, Pop, and the Written Word* (London: Routledge, 1990)

Luke Gibbons, *Transformations in Irish Culture* (Cork: Cork University Press, 1996)

Andrew Goodwin, 'Popular Music and Postmodern Theory', *Cultural Studies*, 5:2 (July 1991), pp. 174–90

Theodor Gracyk, *Rhythm and Noise: An Aesthetics of Rock Music* (London: Duke University Press, 1996)

Bill Graham, *Another Time, Another Place: U2 – The Early Years* (London: Mandarin, 1989)

Dave Harker, *One for the Money: Politics and Popular Song* (London: Hutchinson, 1980)

David Hatch and Stephen Millward, *From Blues to Rock: An Analytical History of Pop Music* (Manchester: Manchester University Press, 1987)

Dermott Hayes, *Sinéad O'Connor: So Different* (London: Omnibus Press, 1991)

Dick Hebdige, *Subculture: The Meaning of Style* (London: Methuen, 1979)

Michael Hicks, *Sixties Rock: Garage, Psychedelia, and Other Satisfactions* (Urbana and Chicago: University of Illinois Press, 1999)

Richard Kearney, *Across the Frontiers: Ireland in the 1990s – Cultural, Political, Economic* (Dublin: Wolfhound Press, 1988)

Kieran Keohane, 'Traditionalism and Homelessness in Contemporary Irish Music', in Jim Mac Laughlin (ed.), *Location and Dislocation in Contemporary Irish Society: Emigration and Irish Identities* (Cork: Cork University Press, 1997), pp. 274–303

Declan Kiberd, 'Modern Ireland: Postcolonial or European?', in Stuart Murray (ed.), *Not on Any Map: Essays on Postcoloniality and Cultural Nationalism* (Exeter: University of Exeter Press, 1997) pp. 81–100

Dave Laing, *One Chord Wonders: Power and Meaning in Punk Rock* (Milton Keynes: Open University Press, 1985)

Dave Laing et al, *The Electric Muse: The Story of Folk into Rock* (London: Methuen, 1975)

J. J Lee, *Ireland 1912–1985: Politics and Society* (Cambridge: Cambridge University Press, 1989)

Brian Longhurst, *Popular Music and Society* (Cambridge: Polity Press, 1995)

Edward Macan, *Rocking the Classics: English Progressive Rock and the Counterculture* (Oxford: Oxford University Press, 1997)

Marie McCarthy, *Passing It On. The Transmission of Music in Irish Culture* (Cork: Cork University Press, 1999)

Noel McLaughlin and Martin McLoone, 'Hybridity and National Musics: The Case of Irish rock Music', *Popular Music* 19:2 (May 2000), pp. 181–200

Avril MacRory, 'The Uncivil War for the soul of Irish Music', *Guardian* (15 December 1995), 2, pp. 8–9

Krister Maim and Roger Wallis, *Media Policy and Music Activity* (London and New York: Routledge, 1992)

Allan F. Moore, *Rock: The Primary Text* (Buckingham: Open University Press, 1993)

Lucy O'Brien, *She Bop: The Definitive History of Women in Rock, Pop and Soul* (London: Penguin, 1995)

Nuala O'Connor, *Bringing It All Back Home: The Influence of Irish Music* (London: BBC Books, 1991)

John J. O'Meara (ed. and trans.), *The History and Topography of Ireland by Gerald of Wales* (1951; London: Penguin, 1982)

Mícheál O Súilleabháin, 'Irish Music Defined', *The Crane Bag* 5:2 (1981), pp. 83–7

Fintan O'Toole, *A Mass for Jesse James: A Journey through 1980's Ireland* (Dublin: Raven Arts Press, 1990)

– *Black Hole, Green Card: The Disappearance of Ireland* (Dublin: New Island Books, 1994)

Richard Pine (ed.), *Music in Ireland 1848–1998* (Cork: Mercier Press, 1998)

Vincent Power, *Send 'Em Home Sweatin': The Showband Story* (1990: rev. edn Cork: Mercier Press, 2000)

Mark J. Prendergast, *Irish Rock: Roots, Personalities, Directions* (Dublin: The O'Brien Press, 1987)

Simon Reynolds and Joy Press, *The Sex Revolts: Gender, Rebellion, and Rock 'n' Roll* (Cambridge, Mass: Harvard University Press, 1995)

Bill Rolston, '"This is not a rebel song": The Irish Conflict and Popular Music', *Race and Class* 42:3 (2001), pp. 49–67

Eddie Rowley, *A Woman's Voice* (Dublin: O'Brien Press, 1993)

Jon Savage, *England's Dreaming: Sex Pistols and Punk Rock* (1991; London: Faber and Faber, 2001)

—, *Time Travel: Pop, Media and Sexuality 1976–96* (London: Chatto and Windus, 1996)

Ann Scanlon, *The Pogues: The Lost Decade* (London: Omnibus Press, 1988)

June Skinner Sawyers, *The Complete Guide to Celtic Music: From the Highland Bagpipe and Riverdance to U2 and Enya* (London: Aurum Press, 2000)

Gerry Smyth, *Space and the Irish Cultural Imagination* (Basingstoke: Palgrave, 2001)

Martin Stokes (ed.), *Ethnicity, Identity and Music: The Musical Construction of Place* (Oxford: Berg, 1994)

Thomas Swiss, John Sloop and Andrew Herman (eds.), *Mapping the Beat: Popular Music and Contemporary Theory* (Oxford: Blackwell, 1998)

Fergal Tobin, *The Best of Decades: Ireland in the 1960s* (Dublin: Gill and Macmillan, 1984)

Fintan Vallely (ed.), *The Companion to Irish Traditional Music* (Cork: Cork University Press, 1999)

Michael Walsh, 'Emerald magic', *Time* 47:11 (11 March 1996), pp. 78–80

John Waters, *Race of Angels: Ireland and the Genesis of U2* (Belfast: Blackstaff Press, 1994)

Harry White, *The Keeper's Recital: Music and Cultural History in Ireland, 1770–1970* (Cork: Cork University Press, 1998)

Sheila Whiteley, *Women and Popular Music: Sexuality, Identity and Subjectivity* (London and New York: Routledge, 2000)

Paul Willis, *Common Culture: Symbolic Work and Play in the Everyday Cultures of the Young* (Buckingham: Open University Press, 1990)

Photo Credits

1964
Them. © John Rodgers/Redferns.

1965
Bluesville. © Ian Whitcomb.
Thanks to Ian Whitcomb.

1966
Dickie Rock. © RTÉ.

1967
The Dubliners. © RTÉ.

1968
Orange Machine. © Deram.
Thanks to Tommy Kinsella.

1969
Eire Apparent. © Buddah.
Thanks to Davy Lutton.

1970
Dr Strangely Strange. © Vertigo.
Thanks to Ivan Pawle.

1971
Skid Row. Photographer: Jorgen Angel.
Thanks to Jorgen Angel.

1972
Mellow Candle. © Deram.
Thanks to Alison O'Donnell and John O'Regan.

1973
Thin Lizzy. © Decca.
Thanks to Phil Osborne and Nick Sharp.

1974
Van Morrison. © David Warner Ellis/Redferns.

1975
Rory Gallagher. © Fin Costello/Redferns.

1976
Horslips. © Gems/Redferns.

1977
The Radiators From Space. Photograph: Nigel
Averill. Thanks to Steve Averill and Pete Holidai.

1978
The Boomtown Rats. © Ian Dickson/Redferns.

1979
Stiff Little Fingers. © Virginia Turbett/Redferns.

1980
The Undertones. Photographer: Larry Doherty.
Thanks to Andy Ferguson and Damian O'Neill.

1981
The Blades. © Reekus.
Thanks to Elvera Butler.

1982
Clannad. © Gered Mankowitz/Redferns.

1983
Paul Brady. © RTÉ.

1984
Microdisney. Photographer: Bleddyn Butcher.
Thanks to Bleddyn Butcher and Judy Toohey.

1985
In Tua Nua. © RTÉ.

1986
The Pogues. Photographer: Steve Pyke.
Thanks to Steve Pyke.

1987
That Petrol Emotion. Photographer: Steve Double.
Thanks to Damian O'Neill.

1988
The Hothouse Flowers. © Martina Raddatz/
Redferns.

1989
The Fat Lady Sings. © Redferns.

1990
Sinead O'Connor. © Mick Hutson/Redferns.

1991
My Bloody Valentine. Photographer: Steve Double.
Thanks to Steve Double.

1992
The Cranberries. © Matt Anker/Retna UK.
Thanks to Simon Sarin.

1993
The Saw Doctors. Photographer: Kyran O'Brien.
Thanks to Larry Hynes and Ollie Jennings.

1994
Aslan. © BMG.
Thanks to Mark Downing.

1995
Whipping Boy. © Redferns.

1996
The Frames. Photographer: Roger Woolman.
Thanks to Roger Woolman.

1997
The Corrs. © Martin Philbey/Redferns.

1998
The Divine Comedy. © Nicky J. Sims/Redferns.

1999
JJ72. Photographer: Roger Woolman.
Thanks to Roger Woolman.

2000
U2. Photographer: Anton Corbijn. © U2 Limited.
Thanks to Anton Corbijn, Candida Bottaci at
Principle, and Louise Butterly, Josie Jones and
Eavann McCarthy at RMP.

2001
Ash. Photographer: Roger Woolman.
Thanks to Roger Woolman.

2002. Gemma Hayes. © Hayley Madden/Redferns.

2003
The Thrills. © Christophe Rihet/Virgin.
Thanks to Victoria Ferrell.

2004
Snow Patrol. Photographer: Gered Mankowitz.
© Polydor Ltd/Fiction. Thanks to Chareen Steel.

Copyright Acknowledgements

Index